Date label overleaf.

SIGN RE
(signs used in the

Good footpath ------ ------ --- ^--^---^-- ---
(sufficiently distinct to be followed in mist)

Intermittent footpath -.-.-.-.-.-.-.-.-.-.-.
(difficult to follow in mist)

Route recommended
but no path ..>.......................>.....
(if recommended one way only, arrow indicates direction)

Wall ∞∞∞∞∞∞∞   Broken wall ∘∘∘∘∘∘∘∘∘∘∘●●

Fence +++++++++++++   Broken fence ׀׀׀׀׀׀׀׀׀׀׀׀׀׀׀׀

Marshy ground ॴॴॴॴॴ   Trees ♤♤♤♤♤♤♤♤

Crags ⣿⣿⣿⣿⣿   Boulders ⬡⬠⬢⬡⬠⬢⬡

Stream or River ∿∿∿∿∿∿∿→
(arrow indicates direction of flow)

Waterfall ⌒⌒⌒↳   Bridge ∿∿✕∿∿

Buildings ▪▪▪   Unenclosed road ▭▭▭▭▭▭

Contours (at 100' intervals) ......1900.....
........1800.....
.....1700.....

Summit-cairn ▲   Other (prominent) cairns △

THE
FAR EASTERN
FELLS

A PICTORIAL GUIDE
TO THE

LAKELAND FELLS

being an illustrated account
of a study and exploration
of the mountains in the
English Lake District

by

A.Wainwright

BOOK TWO
THE FAR EASTERN FELLS

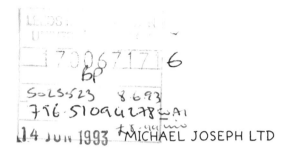
MICHAEL JOSEPH LTD

Published by the Penguin Group
27 Wrights Lane, London W8, England

Penguin Books Ltd Registered Offices:
Harmondsworth, Middlesex, England

First published by Michael Joseph
1992
Originally published by the Westmorland Gazette, 1957

Printed by Titus Wilson and Son, Kendal

ISBN 0 7181 4001 X

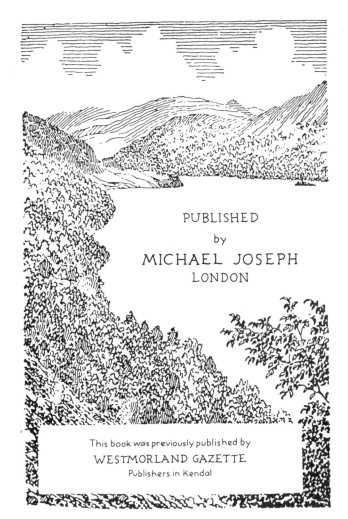

PUBLISHED

by

MICHAEL JOSEPH

LONDON

This book was previously published by

WESTMORLAND GAZETTE

Publishers in Kendal

published 1955
  BOOK ONE : The Eastern Fells

published 1957
  BOOK TWO : The Far Eastern Fells

published 1958
  BOOK THREE : The Central Fells

published 1960
  BOOK FOUR   The Southern Fells

published 1962
  BOOK FIVE : The Northern Fells

published 1964
  BOOK SIX : The North Western Fells

published 1966
  BOOK SEVEN : The Western Fells

Publisher's Note

This book is a re-issue of the original volume written by A. Wainwright. The descriptions of the walks were correct, to the best of A. Wainwright's knowledge, at the time of first publication and are reproduced here without amendment at the wish of the Wainwright Estate. However, since certain footpaths, cairns and other waymarks described here may no longer be accurate, walkers are advised to check with an up-to-date Ordnance Survey map when planning a walk.

BOOK TWO

is dedicated to
the memory of

THE MEN WHO BUILT THE STONE WALLS,

which have endured
the storms of centuries
and remain to this day as monuments to
enterprise perseverance and hard work

Classification and Definition

Any division of the Lakeland fells into geographical districts must necessarily be arbitrary, just as the location of the outer boundaries of Lakeland must always be a matter of opinion. Any attempt to define internal or external boundaries is certain to invite criticism, and he who takes it upon himself to say where Lakeland starts and finishes, or, for example, where the Central Fells merge into the Southern Fells and *which* fells are the Central Fells and which the Southern and *why* they need be so classified, must not expect his pronouncements to be generally accepted.

Yet for present purposes some plan of classification and definition must be used. County and parochial boundaries are no help, nor is the recently-defined area of the Lakeland National Park, for this book is concerned only with the high ground.

First, the external boundaries. Straight lines linking the extremities of the outlying lakes enclose all the higher fells very conveniently. There are a few fells of lesser height to the north and east, however, that are typically Lakeland in character and cannot properly be omitted : these are brought in, somewhat untidily, by extending the lines in those areas. Thus:

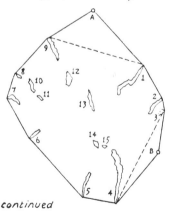

1 : Ullswater
2 : Hawes Water
3 : proposed Swindale Resr
4 : Windermere
5 : Coniston Water
6 : Wast Water
7 : Ennerdale Water
8 : Loweswater
9 : Bassenthwaite Lake
10 : Crummock Water
11 : Buttermere
12 : Derwent Water
13 : Thirlmere
14 : Grasmere
15 : Rydal Water
A : Caldbeck
B : Longsleddale (church)

continued

Classification and Definition

continued   The complete Guide is planned to include all the fells in the area enclosed by the straight lines of the diagram. This is an undertaking quite beyond the compass of a single volume, and it is necessary, therefore, to divide the area into convenient sections, making the fullest use of natural boundaries (lakes, valleys and low passes) so that each district is, as far as possible, self-contained and independent of the rest.

This division gives seven areas, each with a well-defined group of fells, and each will be the subject of a separate volume

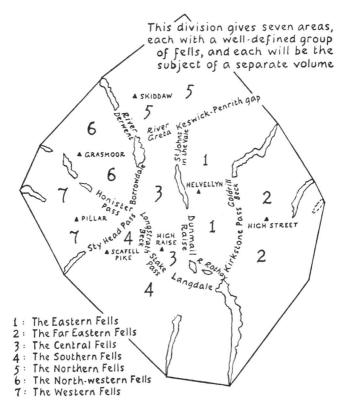

1 : The Eastern Fells
2 : The Far Eastern Fells
3 : The Central Fells
4 : The Southern Fells
5 : The Northern Fells
6 : The North-western Fells
7 : The Western Fells

INTRODUCTION

Notes on the *Illustrations*

THE MAPS................... Many excellent books have been written about Lakeland, but the best literature of all for the walker is that published by the Director General of Ordnance Survey, the 1" map for companionship and guidance on expeditions, the 2½" map for exploration both on the fells and by the fireside. These admirable maps are remarkably accurate topographically but there is a crying need for a revision of the paths on the hills: several walkers' tracks that have come into use during the past few decades, some of them now broad highways, are not shown at all; other paths still shown on the maps have fallen into neglect and can no longer be traced on the ground.

The popular Bartholomew 1" map is a beautiful picture, fit for a frame, but this too is unreliable for paths; indeed here the defect is much more serious, for routes are indicated where no paths ever existed, nor ever could — the cartographer has preferred to take precipices in his stride rather than deflect his graceful curves over easy ground.

Hence the justification for the maps in this book: they have the one merit (of importance to walkers) of being dependable as regards delineation of *paths*. They are intended as supplements to the Ordnance Survey maps, certainly not as substitutes.

THE VIEWS............... Various devices have been used to illustrate the views from the summits of the fells. The full panorama in the form of an outline drawing is most satisfactory generally, and this method has been adopted for the main viewpoints.

THE DIAGRAMS OF ASCENTS................... The routes of ascent of the higher fells are depicted by diagrams that do not pretend to strict accuracy: they are neither plans nor elevations; in fact there is deliberate distortion in order to show detail clearly: usually they are represented as viewed from imaginary 'space-stations.' But it is hoped they will be useful and interesting.

THE DRAWINGS....... The drawings at least are honest attempts to reproduce what the eye sees: they illustrate features of interest and also serve the dual purpose of breaking up the text and balancing the layout of the pages, and of filling up awkward blank spaces, like this:

Thirlmere

THE
FAR EASTERN
FELLS

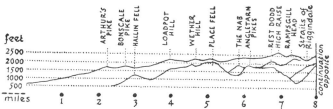

The Far Eastern Fells rise to the east of Kirkstone
Pass and the Patterdale valley, which together form
a natural western boundary to the group. To north
and south these fells run down to low country, and
it is on the east side that difficulty arises in fixing
a demarcation line, for here high ground continues,
to merge ultimately into the Pennines. Nevertheless,
it is possible to adopt a satisfactory boundary, not
so much by a selection of obvious natural features
as by observation of the characteristics of the fells
in this area. Lakeland's fells have a charm that is
unique: they are romantic in atmosphere, dramatic
in appearance, colourful, craggy, with swift-running
sparkling streams and tumbled lichened boulders —
and the walker along this eastern fringe constantly
finds himself passing from the exciting beauty that
is typically Lakeland to the quieter and more sombre
attractiveness that is typically Pennine. Broadly, this
'æsthetic' boundary runs along the eastern watersheds
of Longsleddale, Mosedale and Swindale.

The group has a main spine running through it, due
north and south, that keeps consistently above 2000'
over a distance of eight miles and culminates midway
in the greatest of these fells, High Street. From this
central point there is a general decline in altitude.

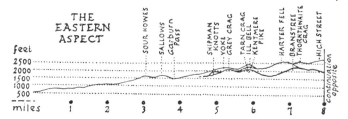

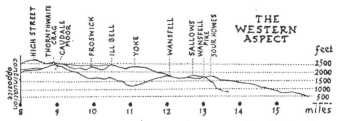

towards the boundaries of the group in all directions
but it is not to be inferred that all ridges radiate
from High Street: on the contrary, it is the pivot of
a complicated system of parallel and lateral ridges
separated by deep valleys that contributes greatly
to the attractiveness of these fells east of Kirkstone.
    The relative inaccessibility of many of the heights
(due to a decided lack of tourist accommodation in
the valleys) can be the only reason why they remain
lonely and unfrequented by visitors, for in the high
quality of the scenery and the excellence of the walks
they rank with the best. In one respect, indeed, they
are supreme, for their extensive and uplifting views
across to the distant Pennines are a delight not to
be found elsewhere in the district. Solitary walkers
will enjoy the area immensely, but they must tread
circumspectly and avoid accident. Mountain-camps
and bivouacs offer the best means of exploration; for
the walker who prefers a bed, Mardale Head used to
be the best centre but now has no hospitality nearer
than the Haweswater Hotel (which is badly sited for
travellers on foot) and the Patterdale valley is most
convenient as a base. The area will be appreciated
best, however, if occasional nights can be arranged
at Howtown, Haweswater, Kentmere and Troutbeck.

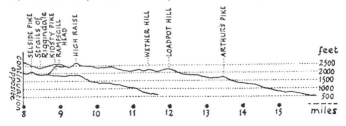

THE FAR EASTERN FELLS

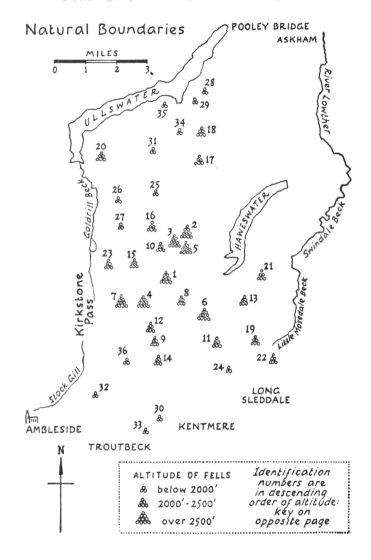

Natural Boundaries

POOLEY BRIDGE
ASKHAM

MILES
0   1   2   3

River Lowther

ULLSWATER

Goldrill Beck

Kirkstone Pass

Stock Gill

AMBLESIDE

N

TROUTBECK

HAWESWATER

Swindale Beck

Little Mosedale Beck

LONG
SLEDDALE

KENTMERE

ALTITUDE OF FELLS
  ஃ below 2000'
  ஃ 2000'–2500'
  ஃ over 2500'

Identification
numbers are
in descending
order of altitude:
key on
opposite page

THE FAR EASTERN FELLS

in the order of
their appearance
in this book

Reference to map opposite: over 2500'	2000'-2500'	below 2000'		Altitude in feet
		26	ANGLETARN PIKES	1857
		28	ARTHUR'S PIKE	1747
		31	BEDA FELL	1664
		29	BONSCALE PIKE	1718
	13		BRANSTREE	2333
		27	BROCK CRAGS	1842
7			CAUDALE MOOR	2502
	12		FROSWICK	2359
	15		GRAY CRAG	2286
	22		GREY CRAG	2093
		35	HALLIN FELL	1271
6			HARTER FELL	2539
	23		HARTSOP DODD	2018
2			HIGH RAISE	2634
1			HIGH STREET	2718
	9		ILL BELL	2476
	11		KENTMERE PIKE	2397
5			KIDSTY PIKE	2560
	10		THE KNOTT	2423
	18		LOADPOT HILL	2201
	8		MARDALE ILL BELL	2496
		25	THE NAB	1887
	20		PLACE FELL	2154
3			RAMPSGILL HEAD	2581
	16		REST DODD	2278
		30	SALLOWS	1691
	21		SELSIDE PIKE	2142
		24	SHIPMAN KNOTTS	1926
		33	SOUR HOWES	1568
		34	STEEL KNOTTS	1414
	19		TARN CRAG	2176
4			THORNTHWAITE CRAG	2569
		36	TROUTBECK TONGUE	1191
		32	WANSFELL	1597
	17		WETHER HILL	2210
	14		YOKE	2309
7	16	13		

36

Each fell is the subject
of a separate chapter

Howtown •

▲ PLACE FELL
• Patterdale
▲ ANGLETARN
PIKES

• Hartsop

HIGH STREET ▲

MILES
0   1   2   3   4

from Brothers Water

NATURAL FEATURES

The distinctive double summit of Angletarn Pikes is a familiar feature high above the Patterdale valley: the two sharp peaks arrest attention from a distance and are no less imposing on close acquaintance, being attainable only by rock-scrambling, easy or difficult according to choice of route. The western flank of the fell drops steeply in slopes of bracken to the pleasant strath of the Goldrill Beck; on this side Dubhow Crag and Fall Crag are prominent. More precipitous is the eastern face overlooking the quiet deer sanctuary of Bannerdale, where the great bastion of Heck Crag is a formidable object rarely seen by walkers. The fell is a part of a broad curving ridge that comes down from the High Street watershed and continues to Boardale Hause, beyond which Place Fell terminates it abruptly.

The crowning glory of the Pikes, however, is the tarn from which they are named, cradled in a hollow just below the summit. Its indented shore and islets are features unusual in mountain tarns, and it has for long, and deservedly, been a special attraction for visitors to Patterdale. The charms of Angle Tarn, at all seasons of the year, are manifold: in scenic values it ranks amongst the best of Lakeland tarns.

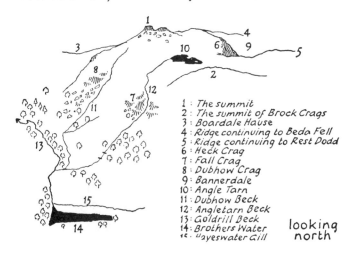

1 : The summit
2 : The summit of Brock Crags
3 : Boardale Hause
4 : Ridge continuing to Beda Fell
5 : Ridge continuing to Rest Dodd
6 : Heck Crag
7 : Fall Crag
8 : Dubhow Crag
9 : Bannerdale
10 : Angle Tarn
11 : Dubhow Beck
12 : Angletarn Beck
13 : Goldrill Beck
14 : Brothers Water
15 : Hayeswater Gill

looking north

Red Screes and Brothers Water from the top of Dubhow Beck

Heck Crag from the Patterdale-Martindale path

ASCENT FROM MARTINDALE
1300 feet of ascent : 3½ miles from Martindale Old Church

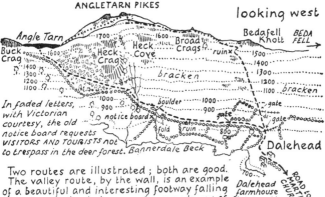

ANGLETARN PIKES

looking west

Angle Tarn 1700 1600 Broad Bedafell BEDA
Buck 1600 Heck Heck Crags Knott FELL
Crag Crag Cove ruin 1500
1400 1400
1300 Bracken 1300
1200 1200 bracken
1100 1100
1000 boulder 1000 gate
In faded letters, 900 900 gate gate
with Victorian notice board fold gate
courtesy, the old 800
notice board requests ruin Dalehead
VISITORS AND TOURISTS not 700
to trespass in the deer forest. Bannerdale Beck

Dalehead
farmhouse
is interesting
architecturally

ROAD TO
MARTINDALE
CHURCH 1½

Two routes are illustrated; both are good.
The valley route, by the wall, is an example
of a beautiful and interesting footway falling
from favour simply because few now know of
it. It ascends the secluded and unfrequented
valley of Bannerdale, passes below Heck Crag
by a sporting path on steep scree and crosses a low saddle to
Angle Tarn, which comes into view suddenly and dramatically:
the highlight of the walk. An easy climb (right) leads to the top.
   The more direct way makes use of the path to Patterdale, but
turns left when the ridge is gained and keeps to the Bannerdale
edge until the summit is close on the right.
   If the return is to be made to Martindale, use the valley route
for the ascent (because of the sudden revelation of Angle Tarn, a
surprise worth planning) and the ridge route for descent.

THE SUMMIT

The north (main) summit

Angle Tarn. from the south summit

Twin upthrusts of rock, 200 yards apart, give individuality to this
unusual summit; the northerly is the higher. Otherwise the top is
generally grassy, with an extensive peat bog in a depression.
DESCENTS : Routes of ascent may be reversed.(Note that, to find
the Bannerdale valley·path, it is necessary first to descend to Angle
Tarn and there cross the low saddle on the left at a boulder opposite
the peninsula). *In mist,* there is comfort in knowing that the path
for Patterdale is only 100 yards distant down the west slope.

THE VIEW

Principal Fells

Although the view is largely confined by surrounding heights to a five-mile radius it is full of interest. The abrupt summit gives splendid depth and fall to the prospect south-west, where there is a beautiful picture of Brothers Water and Kirkstonefoot. Deepdale, directly below, is especially well seen.

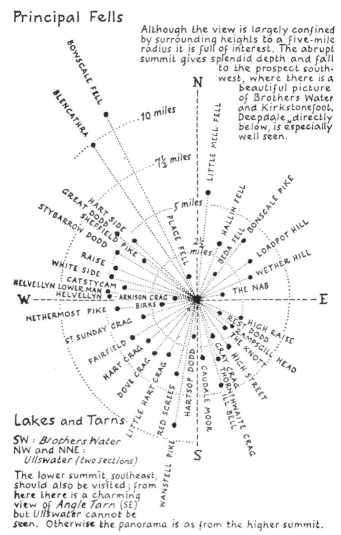

Lakes and Tarns

SW : *Brothers Water*
NW and NNE :
 Ullswater (two sections)

The lower summit, southeast, should also be visited; from here there is a charming view of *Angle Tarn* (SE) but *Ullswater* cannot be seen. Otherwise the panorama is as from the higher summit.

RIDGE ROUTES

To BEDA FELL, 1664' : 2 miles

NE, then N and NE

Main depression at 1450' and several minor depressions

300 feet of ascent

An easy walk, the latter part being dull.

Aim for the high knoll north-east, where an intermittent path leads down a narrowing shoulder (good views of Bannerdale and Heck Crag here). The Patterdale-Martindale path is crossed as it tops the ridge.

Beyond, the walk becomes uninteresting. Beda Fell is dangerous in mist, having precipitous crags on the eastern flank, and the ridge is ill-defined beyond the summit.

The Patterdale-Martindale path is an easy way of escape in bad weather, but must be watched for carefully; it is indistinct as it crosses the ridge.

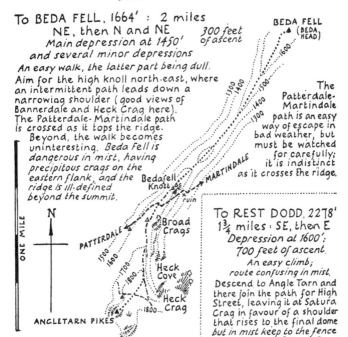

To REST DODD, 2278'

1¾ miles : SE, then E

Depression at 1600': 700 feet of ascent.

An easy climb; route confusing in mist.

Descend to Angle Tarn and there join the path for High Street, leaving it at Satura Crag in favour of a shoulder that rises to the final dome but in mist keep to the fence and wall from Satura Crag.

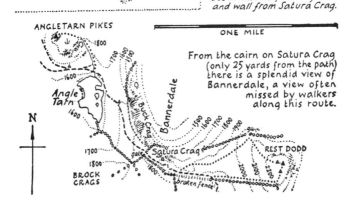

From the cairn on Satura Crag (only 25 yards from the path) there is a splendid view of Bannerdale, a view often missed by walkers along this route.

Pooley Bridge
Askham

▲ ARTHUR'S PIKE

● Howtown

▲ LOADPOT HILL

MILES

0   1   2   3   4

from the Howtown road

NATURAL FEATURES

Arthur's Pike is the northerly termination of the long High Street range, and, like the northerly termination of the parallel Helvellyn range, it contrasts with the usual Lakeland fell-structure by exhibiting its crags to the afternoon sun; the northern and eastern slopes, which are commonly roughest, are without rock. The steep flank falling to Ullswater has several faces of crag below the summit-rim, and, especially around the vicinity of Swarthbeck Gill, which forms the southern boundary of the fell, acres of tumbled boulders testify to the roughness of the impending cliffs and the power of the beck in flood. Above the crags, there is little to excite, and the summit merges without much change in elevation into the broad expanses of Loadpot Hill. The gradual northern slope is clothed with heather.

MAP

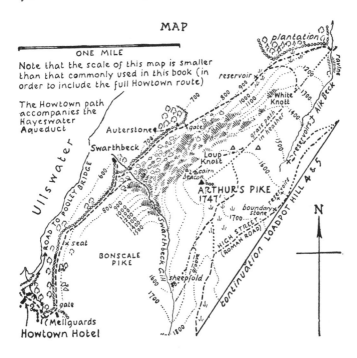

Ullswater, from the Howtown path

ASCENTS

Arthur's Pike looks particularly forbidding from the Howtown path, by which it is usually climbed, and the timid walker who doubts the wisdom of proceeding will be reassured to discover that the ascent is not only not intimidating but surprisingly easy and everywhere pleasant, *if the route shown on the map is followed.* The obvious and direct alternative by the Swarthbeck ravine is anything but obvious and direct when attempted, and nervous pedestrians should keep away from it.

For the approaches from Askham, Helton and Pooley Bridge, the chapter on Loadpot Hill should be consulted.

THE SUMMIT

Above the edge of the steep Ullswater flank, grassy undulations culminate in a conical knoll crowned by a large cairn; nearby is a shelter (from wind) in a short wall. There are no paths on the top, but an indefinite cairned track skirts the precipice, on the brink of which is a collapsed beacon; and on the eastern side is a fairly good path that goes nowhere in particular in either direction and is of little use to the walker. The beacon cannot be seen from the summit-cairn; it stands 250 yards distant in the direction of Blencathra.

THE VIEW

Principal Fells

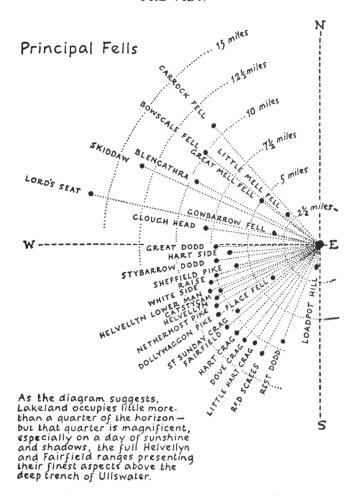

N

15 miles
CARROCK FELL
12½ miles
BOWSCALE FELL
10 miles
LITTLE MELL FELL
7½ miles
SKIDDAW   BLENCATHRA
GREAT MELL FELL
5 miles
LORD'S SEAT
2½ miles
GOWBARROW FELL
CLOUGH HEAD

W - **E**

GREAT DODD
HART SIDE
STYBARROW DODD
SHEFFIELD PIKE
RAISE
WHITE SIDE
HELVELLYN LOWER MAN
CATSTYCAM
HELVELLYN
PLACE FELL
NETHERMOST PIKE
DOLLYWAGGON PIKE
ST SUNDAY CRAG
FAIRFIELD
HART CRAG
DOVE CRAG
LITTLE HART CRAG
RED SCREES
REST DODD
LOADPOT HILL

S

As the diagram suggests,
Lakeland occupies little more
than a quarter of the horizon—
but that quarter is magnificent,
especially on a day of sunshine
and shadows, the full Helvellyn
and Fairfield ranges presenting
their finest aspects above the
deep trench of Ullswater.

Lakes and Tarns

W to N : Ullswater (two sections: middle and lower reaches)
Ullswater is better seen from the beacon : an impressive sight.

RIDGE ROUTES

To LOADPOT HILL, 2201': 2¼ miles
S, then SSW, SSE and finally N
Minor depressions: 500 feet of ascent
A dull, easy walk, not recommended in mist

Aim for the low hill due south, crossing a good path on the way, and join there the old High Street, which is now indistinct in places and at its best only a series of ruts in the grass, often marshy. When the dome of Loadpot Hill is reached, the path becomes an ascending groove, easy to follow; it turns away downhill just short of the ruins of Lowther House, where turn north to the summit-cairn, which encloses a boundary-stone. *This is not a walk for a wet day, and the whole of this moorland is a nightmare in mist.*

To BONSCALE PIKE, 1718'
1 mile: S, then SSW and NW
Depression at 1575'
150 feet of ascent
A simple walk which should not be attempted in mist.

Join the good path running east of the summit and follow it south to a sheepfold in the depression between the two Pikes. Cross the beck and slant over grassy slopes to the right. *Swarthbeck Gill is dangerous below the fold.*

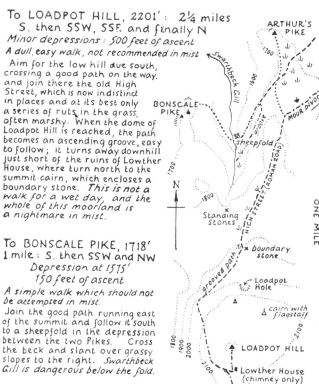

Ullswater, from the beacon

Swarthbeck Gill

Swarthbeck Gill, if it were but more accessible, would be one of the showplaces of the district. Here, between towering rockwalls, are beautiful cataracts, but, alas, they are out of the reach of the average explorer. The ferny, tree-clad lower gorge, however, may (and should) be visited. The prudent venture no further!

Beda Fell

1664'

summit named Beda Head

from Hallin Fell

Beda Fell is the long north-east ridge of Angletarn Pikes, narrowing as it descends; but midway it asserts itself, broadens considerably and rises to a definite summit, Beda Head, which is the geographical centre of the quiet, enchanting, exquisitely beautiful area known affectionately as "Martindʼl." Beyond this top the descent continues over the rocky spine of Winter Crag to valley-level at Sandwick on Ullswater. The fell, although mainly grassy, with bracken, has a most impressive east face, broken into three great tiers of crag. It is bounded by deep valleys, Boardale, Bannerdale and Howe Grain, whose combined waters meet at its northern tip.

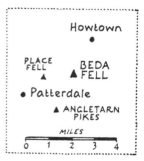

MAP

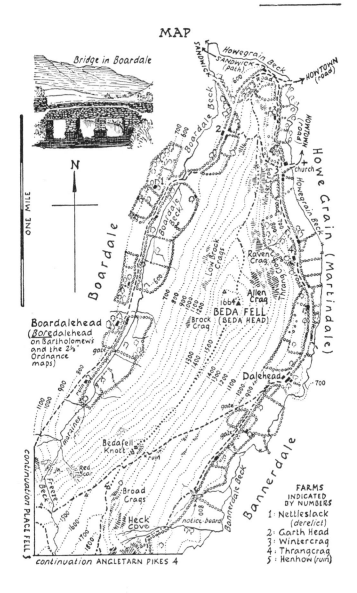

Bridge in Boardale

N

ONE MILE

Boardale

Boardalehead
(*Bore*dalehead
on Bartholomews
and the 2½"
Ordnance
maps)

SANDWICK
Howegrain Beck
SANDWICK (path)
HOWTOWN (road)
HOWTOWN (road)
Howe Grain (Martindale)
church
Howegrain Beck

Boardale Beck
Boardale Beck
Boardale Beck

Raven Crag
Low Brock Crags
Thrang Gill
Allen Crag

1664
BEDA FELL
(BEDA HEAD)
Brock Crag

Dalehead
gate
gate
gate

moraines
ruin

Bedafell Knott
ruin
Red Scar
Broad Crags
Heck Cove
notice-board

Freeze Beck
Bannerdale Beck
Bannerdale

continuation PLACE FELL 3

continuation ANGLETARN PIKES 4

FARMS
INDICATED
BY NUMBERS
1: Nettleslack (derelict)
2: Garth Head
3: Wintercrag
4: Thrangcrag
5: Henhow (ruin)

ASCENTS FROM MARTINDALE AND BOARDALE
1100 feet of ascent : 1¾ miles

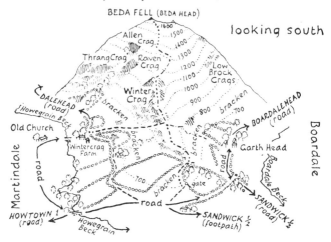

looking south

The fell is best climbed along its north ridge, over the serrated crest of Winter Crag. The ridge may be gained directly at its extremity from the unenclosed road curving round its tip (in high summer, this route involves a tussle with bracken) or by the short paths from Wintercrag Farm and Garth Head. The ridge of Winter Crag is very enjoyable, but the final slope is dreary, although it may be improved by keeping well to the left to look down the crags into Martindale.

DESCENTS : Use the routes of ascent for returning, unless an extension of the walk is desired, in which case the ridge may be continued south-west as far as the Patterdale-Martindale path and a descent made along it.

In mist, exceeding care is necessary to avoid getting entangled among the crags on the east (Martindale) flank, Allen Crag especially being dangerous. In such conditions, it is advisable to descend from the lower cairn, 150 yards northwest, keeping always to the ridge

THE SUMMIT

The highest point, Beda Head, is an uninteresting mound set upon undulating grassy slopes. Infinitely more exciting and attractive is the rocky top of Winter Crag along the ridge.

THE VIEW

Principal Fells

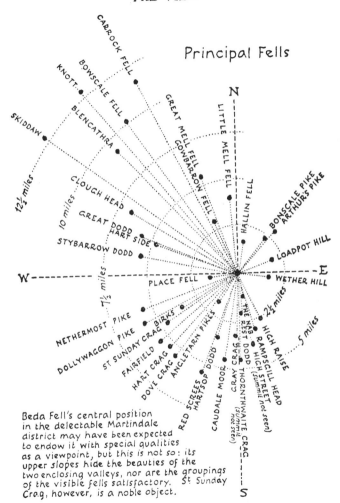

CARROCK FELL
BOWSCALE FELL
KNOTT
SKIDDAW
BLENCATHRA
GREAT MELL FELL
COWBARROW FELL
LITTLE MELL FELL
HALLIN FELL
N
BONSCALE PIKE
ARTHUR'S PIKE
CLOUGH HEAD
12½ miles
10 miles
GREAT DODD
HART SIDE
STYBARROW DODD
LOADPOT HILL
W
7½ miles
PLACE FELL
E
WETHER HILL
NETHERMOST PIKE
DOLLYWAGGON PIKE
BIRKS
ST SUNDAY CRAG
FAIRFIELD
HART CRAG
DOVE CRAG
ANGLETARN PIKES
HARTSOP DODD
THE NAB
THE REST DODD
RAMPSGILL HEAD
HIGH RAISE
2½ miles
5 miles
GRAY CRAG (summit not seen)
HIGH STREET (summit not seen)
THORNTHWAITE CRAG (summit not seen)
RED SCREES
CAUDALE MOOR
S

Beda Fell's central position
in the delectable Martindale
district may have been expected
to endow it with special qualities
as a viewpoint, but this is not so: its
upper slopes hide the beauties of the
two enclosing valleys, nor are the groupings
of the visible fells satisfactory. St Sunday
Crag, however, is a noble object.

Lakes and Tarns

N to NE : *Ullswater* (two sections, divided by *Hallin Fell*)

RIDGE ROUTE

To ANGLETARN PIKES, 1857'
2 miles : SW, then S and SW
Main depression at 1450'
and several minor depressions

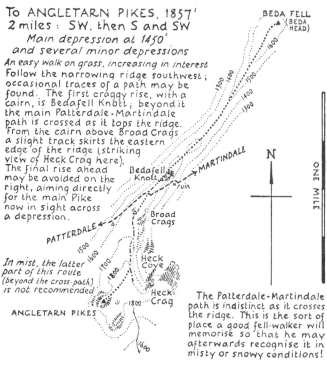

An easy walk on grass, increasing in interest
Follow the narrowing ridge southwest;
occasional traces of a path may be
found. The first craggy rise, with a
cairn, is Bedafell Knott; beyond it
the main Patterdale-Martindale
path is crossed as it tops the ridge.
From the cairn above Broad Crags
a slight track skirts the eastern
edge of the ridge (striking
view of Heck Crag here).
The final rise ahead
may be avoided on the
right, aiming directly
for the main Pike
now in sight across
a depression.

*In mist, the latter
part of this route
(beyond the cross-path)
is not recommended*

N

ONE MILE

BEDA FELL
(BEDA HEAD)

MARTINDALE

Bedafell Knott

ruin

PATTERDALE

Broad Crags

Heck Cove

Heck Crag

ANGLETARN PIKES

The Patterdale-Martindale
path is indistinct as it crosses
the ridge. This is the sort of
place a good fell-walker will
memorise so that he may
afterwards recognise it in
misty or snowy conditions!

The ridge south from the cairn
above Broad Crags; on the right
the main Angletarn Pike.

Beda Fell
from
Martindale Old Church

Bonscale Pike

1718'

sometimes referred to as
Swarth Fell

named Toughmoss Pike
on Bartholomew's map

from Hallin Fell

- • Pooley Bridge

▲ ARTHUR'S PIKE
▲ **BONSCALE PIKE**
• Howtown
▲ LOADPOT HILL

MILES
0 1 2 3 4

NATURAL FEATURES

Rising steeply behind the little hamlet of Howtown is a broad buttress of the High Street range, Swarth Fell, the turretted and castellated rim of which has the appearance, when seen from Ullswater far below, of the ruined battlements of a castle wall: this aspect is sufficiently arresting to earn for the rocky facade and the summit above it the separate and distinctive name of Bonscale Pike. This escarpment, however, is a sham, for it defends nothing other than a dreary plateau of grass; and indeed there is little else of interest on the fell — excepting Swarthbeck Gill, its northern boundary, which abounds in interest but is out of bounds for the walker because of its obvious dangers. Bonscale Pike presents a bold front, that overlooking the lake, but on all other sides it loses its identity in the high mass of land supporting the great dome of Loadpot Hill.

MAP

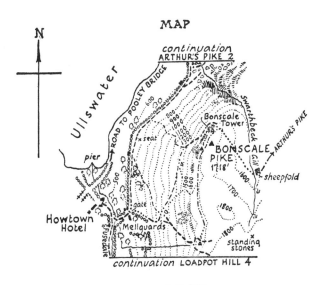

ONE MILE

ASCENT FROM HOWTOWN
1200 feet of ascent : 1¼ miles

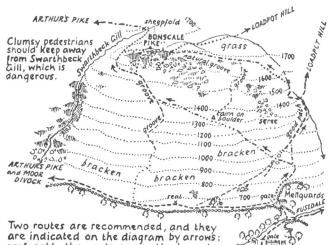

ARTHUR'S PIKE ←--- sheepfold 1700 LOADPOT HILL

Clumsy pedestrians should keep away from Swarthbeck Gill, which is dangerous.

BONSCALE PIKE   grass   LOADPOT HILL

natural groove

groove   1700

1600

1500

groove   1400

cairn on boulder   scree

1400   goat path

1300

1200

1100   bracken

1000

ARTHUR'S PIKE and MOOR DIVOCK   bracken   900

bracken   800

seat   700   gate   Mellguards

FUSEDALE

gate   Howtown Hotel

Two routes are recommended, and they are indicated on the diagram by arrows: preferably, the route across the breast should be used for ascent and that south along the top for descent.

looking east·south·east

The work of a craftsman
Bonscale Tower

The effort of amateurs
The higher pillar

THE SUMMIT

Neither of the two stone pillars seen so prominently against the skyline from below marks the highest point, this being a grassy hummock between and behind them, with a small cairn. It is an unsatisfactory summit because higher ground rises immediately beyond on the long undulating slope to Loadpot Hill; it does, however, indicate an excellent viewpoint, and also defines the limit of interest, which is centred in the broken wall of crag immediately below. Bonscale Pike, in fact, gives a display of rock-scenery that would improve many a bigger fell.   And the men who selected the sites for the two pillars surely had a good appreciation of drama!

DESCENTS: The alternative route of ascent should be used as a way down in order to get the full benefit of the views, but in any case the length of the summit should be traversed.

In mist, a stranger may well feel cause for anxiety. The lower (in altitude), i.e. the northerly, of the two pillars should be rounded above it, by an ample margin, to reach the path below the crags, after which the slope may safely be descended anywhere if the path is lost. Note that the two pillars both stand on the brink of crags.   Resist any temptation to slant down to the stream — Swarthbeck Gill is highly dangerous.

Plan of the summit

THE VIEW

Principal Fells

The distant fell peeping over the skyline, right of Arthur's Pike, is Cross Fell the highest of the Pennines

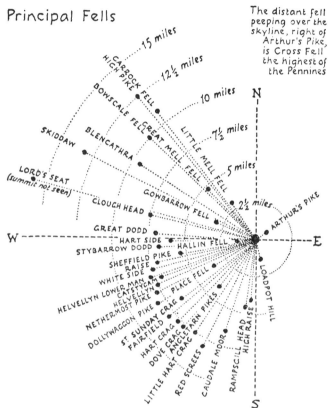

The prospect of the Helvellyn and Fairfield ranges, although crowded into a quarter-circle, is excellent, and the more distant northern fells are nicely grouped. In other directions there is little to be seen but the nearby dreary slopes falling from Loadpot Hill. The pillars are better viewpoints.

Lakes and Tarns

W to N: Ullswater
(middle and lower reaches)
— better seen from either of the two pillars

RIDGE ROUTES

To ARTHUR'S PIKE, 1747': 1 mile
SE, then NNE and N
Depression at 1575'
200 feet of ascent
A simple walk, needing care in mist
Slant down a grass slope *south-east*
to the beck, crossing it above a
sheepfold and doubling back
along the opposite slope, where
a fair path will be joined : this
path skirts the summit, and
must be left to visit the cairn.
Short cuts across Swarthbeck Gill,
especially in mist, are dangerous.

To LOADPOT HILL, 2201': 1½ miles
S, then SSE and finally N
Minor depressions
550 feet of ascent
An easy walk, not recommended in mist
Cross the undulating plateau
southwards until the ground
steepens into the vast dome
of Loadpot Hill. A short climb
brings the old High Street (a
grassy groove) underfoot: it
leads to the ruins of Lowther
House, where turn north to
the handsome cairn.

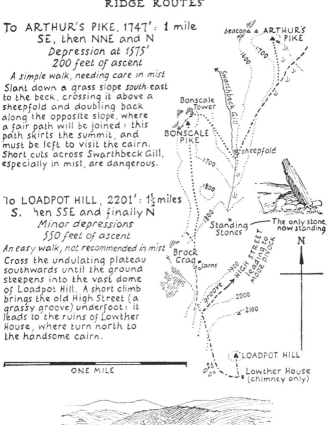

ONE MILE

Ullswater:
the middle reach

Branstree

2333'

(a corruption of Brant Street)
The summit is not named
on Ordnance Survey maps

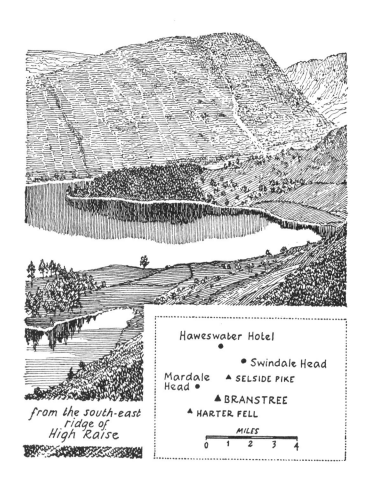

*from the south-east
ridge of
High Raise*

Haweswater Hotel
●

● Swindale Head

Mardale
Head ●

▲ SELSIDE PIKE

▲ BRANSTREE

▲ HARTER FELL

MILES

0 1 2 3 4

NATURAL FEATURES

Branstree occupies a fine position at the head of three valleys, Mardale, Swindale and Longsleddale, and a fourth, Mosedale, runs along its southern base. This geographical attribute aside, the fell is dreary, and must disappoint all who climb it, for a good deal of perambulation is necessary across the flat and featureless top before these valleys can be brought sufficiently into view for full appreciation. All is grass, although there is a slight boulder-slope below Artlecrag Pike (extravagantly hachured as a crag on most maps), and a remarkable dry gully, the result of a landslide, cleaves the fellside on the Mardale flank from top to bottom. Eastwards there are some subsidiary summits, and a line of crags overlooking Swindale; there is an odd little hanging valley, and noble hidden waterfalls on this side. The Mosedale flank has been extensively quarried. Mosedale Beck is the principal stream : it runs into Swindale Beck, on which Manchester Corporation have covetous eyes.

High Street
from the north ridge

MAP

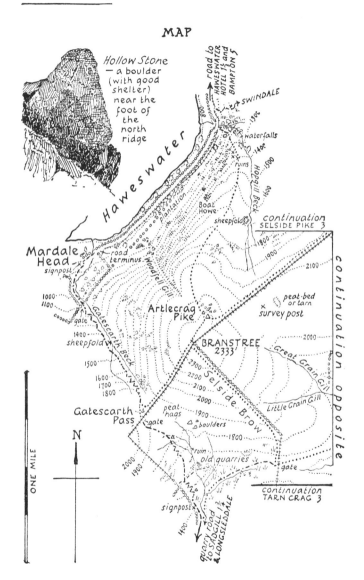

Hollow Stone — a boulder (with good shelter) near the foot of the north ridge

road to HAWESWATER HOTEL 1½ and BAMPTON 5

SWINDALE

waterfalls

ruins

Hopgill Beck

HAWESWATER

Boat Howe

sheepfold

continuation
SELSIDE PIKE 3

Mardale Head

signpost

road terminus

plantation

Woodell Gill

peat bed or tarn

× survey post

Artlecrag Pike

gate

sheepfold

Gatescarth Beck

BRANSTREE 2333'

Selside Brow

Great Grain Gill

Little Grain Gill

continuation opposite

Gatescarth Pass

peat hags

gate

boulders

ruin

old quarries

gate

N

signpost

quarry road to SADGILL 1¼ & LONGSLEDDALE

continuation
TARN CRAG 3

ONE MILE

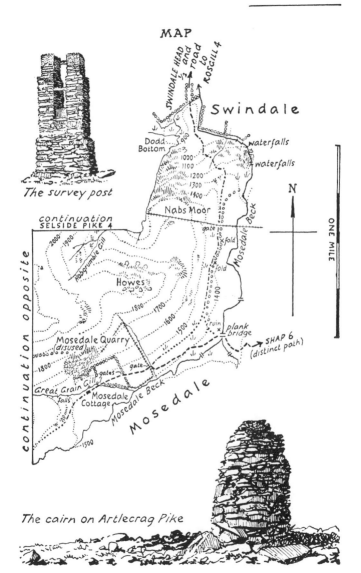

MAP

The survey post

Swindale

SWINDALE HEAD and road to ROSGILL 4

Dodd Bottom

waterfalls

waterfalls

900

1000

1100

1200

1300

1400

Nabs Moor

N

ONE MILE

gate

fold

fold

Mosedale Beck

continuation SELSIDE PIKE 4

2000

1900

Hobgrumble Gill

Howes

1800

1700

1600

1500

1400

continuation opposite

Mosedale Quarry
(disused)

1800

gate

gates

ruin

plank
bridge

SHAP 6
(distinct path)

Great Grain Gill

falls

Mosedale
Cottage

Mosedale Beck

Mosedale

1500

The cairn on Artlecrag Pike

ASCENT FROM MARDALE
1500 feet of ascent : 1½ miles from the road

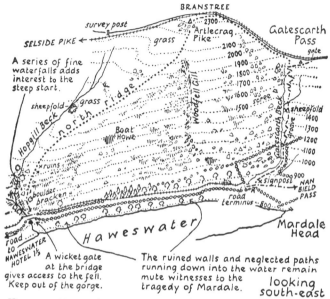

A series of fine waterfalls adds interest to the steep start.

A wicket gate at the bridge gives access to the fell. Keep out of the gorge.

The ruined walls and neglected paths running down into the water remain mute witnesses to the tragedy of Mardale.

looking south-east

The merit of the ascent by the north ridge lies in its intimate views of Mardale Head and Harter Fell, the climbing itself being dull after a promising start. The Gatescarth route is better used for the return.

ASCENT FROM LONGSLEDDALE

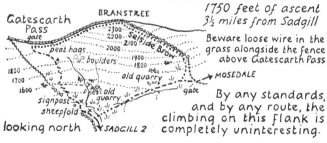

1750 feet of ascent 3½ miles from Sadgill

Beware loose wire in the grass alongside the fence above Gatescarth Pass

looking north

By any standards, and by any route, the climbing on this flank is completely uninteresting.

THE SUMMIT

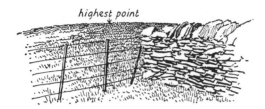

highest point

The 'official' watershed is about eighty yards north of the end of the wall; this is the highest point (2333')

The summit is grassy and flat-topped. There is no cairn on the highest point, which is situated near the junction of a well-built wall and the wire fence that traverses the fell. A better place for a halt is the fine cairn on Artlecrag Pike nearby, north-east; here also is some rock to relieve the drab surroundings.

DESCENTS: The quickest way off, and the safest in bad weather, is by the fence to Gatescarth Pass (beware loose wire in the grass, and watch for the gate that indicates the path for Longsleddale, left, and Mardale, right). The most attractive descent is that by the north ridge for Mardale, with good views of Haweswater.

RIDGE ROUTE

TO TARN CRAG, 2176'
1¾ miles : SE, then S
Depression at 1650'
550 feet of ascent
Easy gradients ; a dull walk
Features of interest are lacking on this moorland trudge. Care is needed on Tarn Crag in mist.

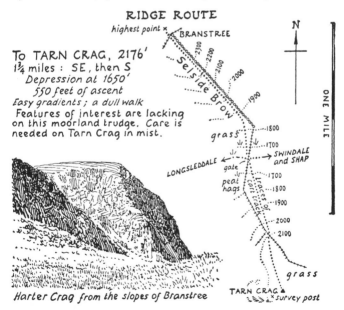

Harter Crag from the slopes of Branstree

RIDGE ROUTES

To HARTER FELL, 2539': 2 miles: SW then NW and SW
Depression at 1875' (Gatescarth Pass): 700 feet of ascent
An easy walk on grass. Safe in mist, with care

Loose wire alongside the fence going down to Gatescarth Pass is a snare for the unsuspecting walker, especially he who travels at speed. When the fence turns, continue along the line marked by the fragmentary remains of an old fence, which can be traced to the summit. In mist, this line must be followed carefully.

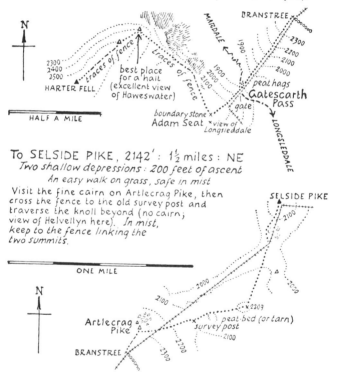

To SELSIDE PIKE, 2142': 1½ miles: NE
Two shallow depressions: 200 feet of ascent
An easy walk on grass, safe in mist

Visit the fine cairn on Artlecrag Pike, then cross the fence to the old survey post and traverse the knoll beyond (no cairn; view of Helvellyn here). In mist, keep to the fence linking the two summits.

The survey post was built by Manchester Corporation during the construction of the Haweswater Aqueduct. It does not stand on the crest of the depression, as might have been expected, but slightly below it; the top of the post, however, overtops the crest and the next survey post, on Tarn Crag, is visible from it (south).

THE VIEW

Principal Fells

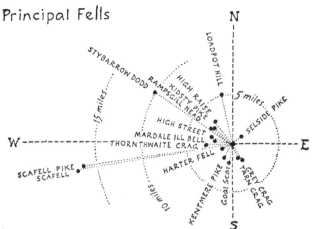

Lakes and Tarns

Branstree is one of the very few Lakeland fells that have no view of lakes or tarns from the highest point, but Haweswater is brought into view by walking a few paces north. The long strip of water in the distance southwards is the Kent estuary.

Despite Branstree's good geographical position, little is seen of Lakeland: the lofty skyline of the Mardale heights admits only two small vistas of distant fells. Compensation is found, however, in the wide prospect of the Pennines. An interesting feature is the glimpse of the Scafells with Mickledore — note that, of this group, only the Pike is in view from the wall end.

Mosedale Cottage — occasionally occupied by shepherds

Brock Crags

1842'

from Goldrill Beck

The unspoilt village of Low Hartsop has great charm and its environment is one of quiet loveliness, much of it contributed by the hanging woods of the steep fell that rises immediately behind. This fell, Brock Crags, is an offshoot of a ridge coming down to Ullswater from the main High Street watershed, and overlooks a meeting of many valleys: a feature in the view from the rocky top. Its slopes carry the Hayeswater aqueduct, and recent pipelaying operations there have left an ugly scar along its fair breast. Nature is a great healer: it cannot heal too swiftly here.

MAP

continuation
ANGLETARN PIKES 4
PATTERDALE 2

PATH to PATTERDALE 1½

ROAD TO PATTERDALE 1¾

Goldrill Beck

Angle Tarn

Fall Crag

Angletarn Beck

Cal Crag

falls

Calf Close

Lingy Crag

BROCK CRAGS
1842

gate

gate

REST DODD

1600
1700
1800
1500
1400
1300

line of aqueduct

Low Hartsop

filter house

Brothers Water

ROAD to KIRKSTONE PASS

Hayeswater Gill

old shaft

→ HAYESWATER 1

N

ONE MILE

ASCENT FROM HARTSOP
1300 feet of ascent : 1 mile

The exit from Hartsop is not clear. Either (a) start along a lane opposite a turning-space for cars near the end of the village, soon bearing right along a grass path between walls (ignore the road going left) and then uphill across an enclosure to the pipeline. Or (b) follow the cart-track up the valley to the filter-house, turning back along the pipeline at a higher level. Above the pipeline, find a grooved path ascending right through a gap in an old wall: it becomes indistinct at 1600', the summit then being over easy slopes to the left. Or follow the old wall straight up.

Iron gateposts are met on the grooved path at 1500', remnants of a vanished fence

But the great unnatural feature on this walk is the pipeline scar, which distinctly offends!

BROCK CRAGS

Shelter under crag

1800
1700
1600
1500
1400
1300
1200
1100

old wall

grooved path

Hayeswater Aqueduct

1000 Pipeline

filter house

Pipeline

road

900
800

pastures

gate

cart-track

Hayeswater Gill

Hartsop

gate

looking north

Brock Crags 3

THE SUMMIT

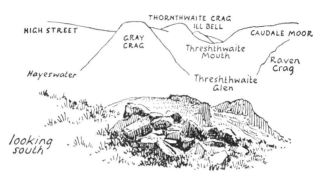

looking south

A series of rocky knolls, on the highest of which is a cairn, adds some interest to the rather drab surroundings. It is as a viewpoint that the summit merits most respect.

DESCENTS: A quick descent to Hartsop may be made by following downhill the old wall that crosses the fellside 150 yards south-east; descents due west encounter rough ground and should not be attempted. For Patterdale the Angle Tarn path may be joined near the Satura Crag gate by following the old wall eastwards. *In bad weather, locate the wall and follow it down to the pastures of Hartsop.*

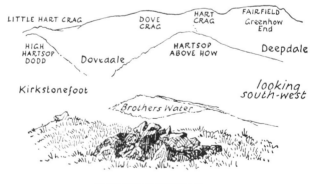

looking south-west

RIDGE ROUTES

Brock Crags stands apart from the ridge that links Rest Dodd with Angletarn Pikes. To join the ridge, for either of these fells, follow the old wall eastwards to the gate on Satura Crag, where the connecting path will be found

THE VIEW

Principal Fells

The scene is interesting, with a fine surround of higher fells; in particular the bird's-eye view of Brothers Water and Hartsop is beautiful and dramatic

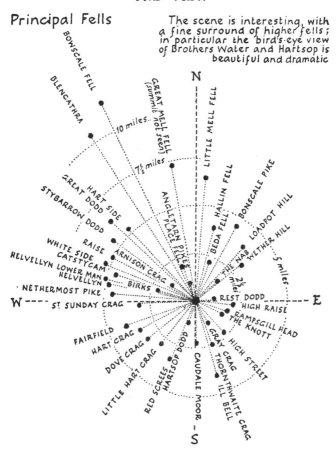

Lakes and Tarns

N : Angle Tarn
SE : Hayeswater
SW : Brothers Water
NW : Ullswater

Caudale Moor 2502'

often referred to as
  John Bell's Banner
summit named
  Stony Cove Pike

• Patterdale

• Hartsop

HIGH
STREET ▲

CAUDALE ▲ MOOR

▲ RED SCREES

• Ambleside

MILES
0 1 2 3 4

from Brothers Water

NATURAL FEATURES

Caudale Moor deserves far more respect than it usually gets. The long featureless slope flanking the Kirkstone Pass, well known to travellers, is not at all characteristic of the fell : its other aspects, less frequently seen, are considerably more imposing. There are, in fact, no fewer than six ridges leaving the summit in other directions, four of them of distinct merit and two of these rising to subsidiary summits, Wansfell and Hartsop Dodd, on their way to valley-level. The craggy slopes bordering the upper Troutbeck valley are particularly varied and interesting : from this remote dalehead Caudale Moor looks really impressive, especially in snowy conditions. The best single feature, however, is the formidable wall of rock, Raven Crag, overlooking Pasture Beck. Of the streams draining the fell, those to the south join forces to form Trout Beck ; all others go north to feed Ullswater.

looking west

1 : The summit (Stony Cove Pike)
2 : Hartsop Dodd
3 : St. Raven's Edge
4 : Main south ridge
    continuing to Wansfell
5 : Hart Crag
6 : Pike How
7 : Intermediate south ridge
8 : South ridge (east)
9 : North-west ridge
10 : North ridge
11 : East ridge
12 : Threshthwaite Mouth
13 : Raven Crag
14 : Woundale Beck
15 : Trout Beck
16 : Sad Gill
17 : Pasture Beck

The six ridges of Caudale Moor

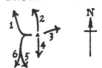

1 : North-west (to Brothers Water)
2 : North (to Hartsop)
3 : East (to Thornthwaite Crag
        or Hartsop or Troutbeck)
4 : South (east) (to Troutbeck)
5 : South (intermediate)
        (to Troutbeck)
6 : South (west) (to Kirkstone)

MAP

continuation on opposite page

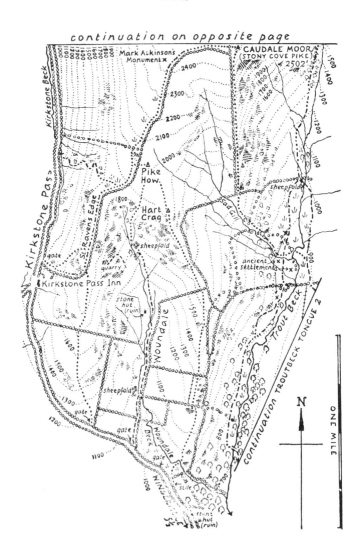

MAP

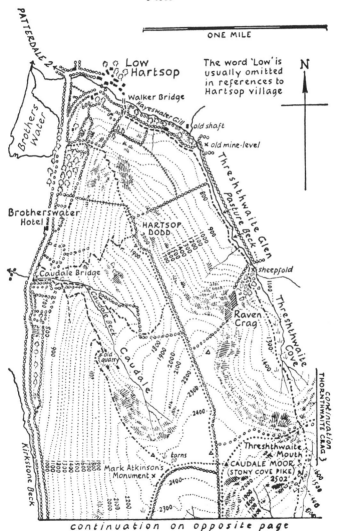

ONE MILE

The word 'Low' is usually omitted in references to Hartsop village

N

PATTERDALE 2

Low Hartsop

Brothers Water

Walker Bridge

Hayeswater Gill

old shaft

x old mine-level

Threshthwaite Glen

Pasture Beck

Brotherswater Hotel

HARTSOP DODD

Caudale Bridge

Caudale Beck

Caudale

old quarry

sheepfold

Raven Crag

Threshthwaite Cove

CONTINUATION THORNTHWAITE CRAGS 3

Kirkstone Beck

Mark Atkinson's Monument x

tarns

Threshthwaite Mouth

CAUDALE MOOR (STONY COVE PIKE) 2502

continuation on opposite page

ASCENT FROM KIRKSTONE PASS
1150 feet of ascent : 2½ miles from the Inn

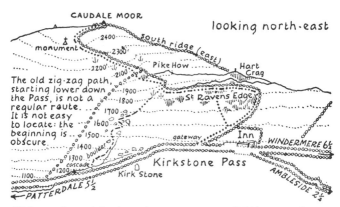

CAUDALE MOOR

looking north·east

2400

monument 2300

2200 Pike How

South ridge (east)

Hart Crag

2100

St Ravens Edge

1900

1800

The old zig·zag path, starting lower down the Pass, is not a regular route. It is not easy to locate: the beginning is obscure.

1700
1600
1500
1400

gateway

Inn

WINDERMERE 6½

1300 boulder
cascade 1200

Kirk Stone

Kirkstone Pass

AMBLESIDE 2½

1100

← PATTERDALE 5½

This route, with the advantage of a 1500' start, is one of the easiest ways up any of the higher fells, the only steep part being the short pull on to St Ravens Edge. It is also the *dullest* way up, and does not do justice to a fine hill that has much better than this to offer.

Caudale Moor
from
below Scot Rake

ASCENT FROM BROTHERS WATER
2000 feet of ascent: 2½ miles from the Hotel

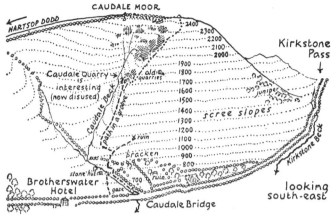

CAUDALE MOOR

HARTSOP DODD

2400
2300
2200
2100
2000
1900
1800
1700
1600
1500
1400
1300
1200
1100
1000
900
800
700

Kirkstone Pass ↓

Caudale Quarry
is
interesting
(now disused)

old
quarries

Caudale beck

Path narrows

scree slopes

juniper

× ruin

bracken

stone hut

gate

× ruin

Kirkstone Beck

Brotherswater Hotel

Caudale Bridge

looking south-east

The beautiful retrospect over Patterdale is justification
for frequent halts during this continuously steep ascent.
The route follows the well-defined crest of the ridge. Of
the many approaches to the summit, this is by far the best.

Threshthwaite Cove
from
Threshthwaite Mouth

ASCENT FROM TROUTBECK
2200 (A) **or** 2350 (B) feet of ascent;
(A) 5 miles via Sad Gill; 5½ miles via Woundale (A)
(B) 6 miles via St Ravens Edge or Threshthwaite Mouth (B)

looking north

Both Trout Beck (below its attractive slate bridge — which few artists know but all would love) and Sad Gill (in several places) run along small rocky ravines

Of the various routes illustrated, only that by Sad Gill (reached via either side of the Tongue) and the ridge above it can be recommended without qualification; this climb has merit, but the other routes are dull.

The valley of the Trout Beck west of the Tongue is very pretty, but the ground beyond the bridge is wet: the path keeps well away from the beck. The east side of the Tongue has a dry and excellent track

THE SUMMIT

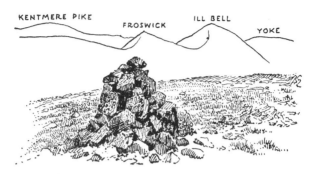

KENTMERE PIKE   FROSWICK   ILL BELL   YOKE

The summit is a dreary plateau of considerable extent, crossed by stone walls, with grey rock outcropping in the wide expanse of grass. The highest point is not easy to locate on the flat top: it is indicated by a cairn, *east of the north-south wall*, and bears the distinctive name of Stony Cove Pike.

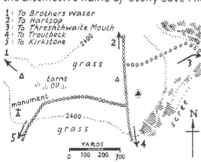

1: To Brothers Water
2: To Hartsop
3: To Threshthwaite Mouth
4: To Troutbeck
5: To Kirkstone

grass

tarns

monument

scree

2400

2400

YARDS
0   100   200   300

N

Mark Atkinson's Monument

DESCENTS: All routes of ascent may be reversed in good weather. There are no paths on the top, but (excepting the north-west ridge) accompanying walls are safe guides from the summit.

In bad weather, note that the east face is everywhere craggy: it may be descended safely *only* by the broken wall going down to the Threshthwaite gap. The best way off the top in an emergency, whatever the destination, is alongside the wall running west — this continues without a break to the road near Kirkstone Pass Inn.

Cairn above the north-west ridge

THE VIEW

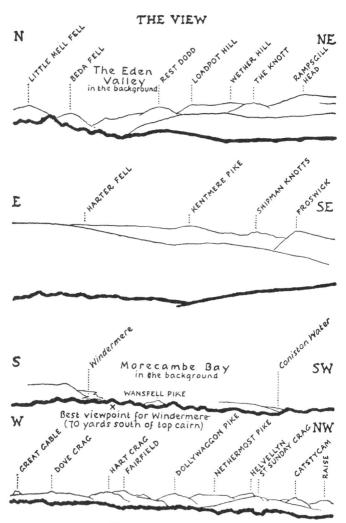

The view in this direction
is much better seen from
the western edge of the summit-plateau

THE VIEW

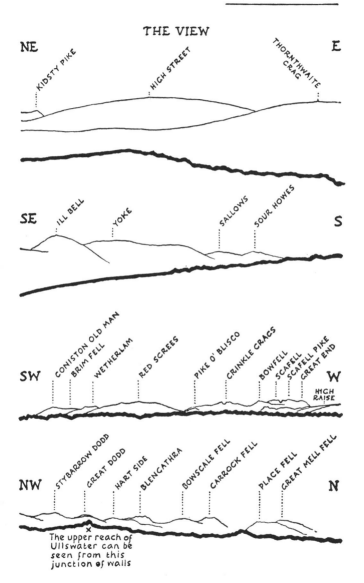

NE

KIDSTY PIKE
HIGH STREET
THORNTHWAITE CRAG

E

SE

ILL BELL
YOKE
SALLOWS
SOUR HOWES

S

SW

CONISTON OLD MAN
BRIM FELL
WETHERLAM
RED SCREES
PIKE O' BLISCO
CRINKLE CRAGS
BOWFELL
SCAFELL
SCAFELL PIKE
GREAT END
HIGH RAISE

W

NW

STYBARROW DODD
GREAT DODD
HART SIDE
BLENCATHRA
BOWSCALE FELL
CARROCK FELL
PLACE FELL
GREAT MELL FELL

N

The upper reach of
Ullswater can be
seen from this
junction of walls

RIDGE ROUTE

To WANSFELL, 1597': 4½ miles: W, then SW and S
Depression at 1100': 500 feet of ascent

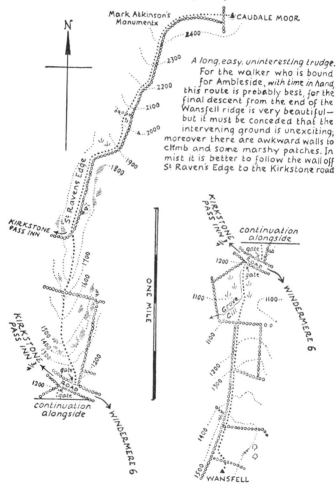

A long, easy, uninteresting trudge.
For the walker who is bound
for Ambleside, with time in hand,
this route is probably best, for the
final descent from the end of the
Wansfell ridge is very beautiful—
but it must be conceded that the
intervening ground is unexciting;
moreover there are awkward walls to
climb and some marshy patches. In
mist it is better to follow the wall off
St Raven's Edge to the Kirkstone road

RIDGE ROUTES

To THORNTHWAITE CRAG, 2569': 1 mile: ENE, then E and SE
Depression at 1950': 620 feet of ascent
A rough scramble, safe in mist

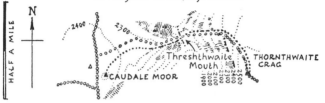

This walk is not as simple as it looks, because the deep gap or col (Threshthwaite Mouth) between the two fells is unsuspected from the top of Caudale Moor. The descent to the gap is steep (if there is snow and ice it may be dangerous) and the climb from it is stony and loose. In mist, it is important to keep alongside the crumbled wall that links the two summits.

To HARTSOP DODD, 2018': 1⅓ miles: N, then NNW
Depression at 1900': 120 feet of ascent
An easy, straightforward walk

The wall running north is a dull companion to Hartsop Dodd; it is better to follow the escarpment on the right for the sake of the striking views down into Threshthwaite.

Cairn on Hart Crag above Woundale

Ullswater and Brothers Water
from Caudale Quarry

Red Screes and Middle Dodd
from the north-west ridge

Caudale Head

Raven Crag

Froswick

2359'

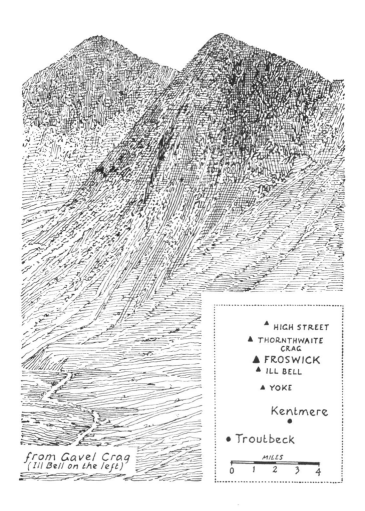

from Gavel Crag
(Ill Bell on the left)

▲ HIGH STREET

▲ THORNTHWAITE
    CRAG

▲ FROSWICK

▲ ILL BELL

▲ YOKE

Kentmere
•

• Troutbeck

MILES
0   1   2   3   4

NATURAL FEATURES

Sheltering in the shadow of Ill Bell on High Street's south ridge is the lesser height of Froswick. It takes its pattern from Ill Bell in remarkable degree, almost humorously seeming to ape its bigger neighbour. Both flanks are very steep, the Kentmere side especially being a rough tumble of scree: there are crags here facing up the valley. The grassy Troutbeck slope, west, is notable for Froswick's one touch of originality, for it is cleft by a tremendous scree gully, Blue Gill, that splits the fellside from top to bottom. Easy slopes link the summit with Thornthwaite Crag and Ill Bell; this is the finest part of the ridge.

MAP

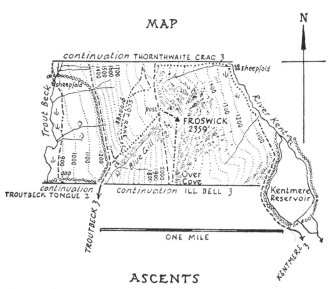

ASCENTS

Froswick is rarely climbed direct; invariably its summit is gained incidentally during the course of the Ill Bell ridge-walk, starting at Garburn Pass. From Troutbeck, however, its top may be visited on the way to High Street by Scot Rake, in which case it is quicker to climb alongside Blue Gill than to waste time trying to locate Scot Rake. A direct ascent from Kentmere is not recommended, this flank being steep, loose and unpleasant, although the ridge north of the summit may be reached up a continuous tongue of grass from the sheepfold,

THE SUMMIT

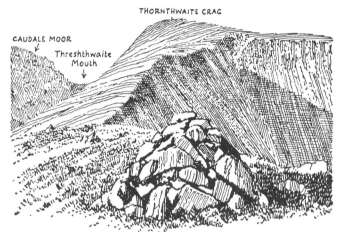

THORNTHWAITE CRAG

CAUDALE MOOR

Threshthwaite Mouth

Froswick's peaked appearance from afar holds out the promise of a small pointed summit. Small it is, and neat, with a tidy cairn, but it will hardly satisfy the seeker of spires.
DESCENTS: The routes of ascent may be reversed. The western flank is safe anywhere (but keep out of Blue Gill); do not attempt the *direct* descent to Kentmere. *In mist*, reach Kentmere by way of Garburn Pass.

RIDGE ROUTES

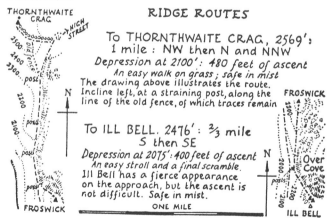

To THORNTHWAITE CRAG, 2569':
1 mile : NW then N and NNW
Depression at 2100': 480 feet of ascent
An easy walk on grass ; safe in mist
The drawing above illustrates the route.
Incline left, at a straining post, along the
line of the old fence, of which traces remain

To ILL BELL, 2476': ⅔ mile
S then SE
Depression at 2075': 400 feet of ascent
An easy stroll and a final scramble.
Ill Bell has a fierce appearance
on the approach, but the ascent is
not difficult. Safe in mist.
ONE MILE

THE VIEW

Sandwiched between Thornthwaite Crag
and Ill Bell, both higher, Froswick
is an undistinguished viewpoint,
the best feature being the
serrated skyline of the
Scafell and Langdale
heights in the west

Principal Fells

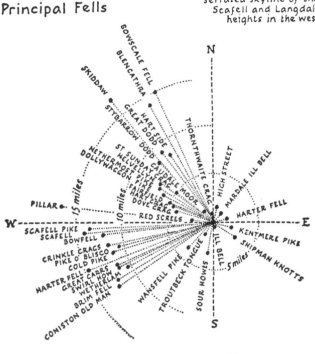

*Ill Bell
from
Froswick*

Lakes and Tarns
SE : *Kentmere Reservoir*
SSW : *Windermere*
NNW : *Ullswater*

Gray Crag

2286'

Hartsop
▲ GRAY CRAG
▲ HIGH
STREET
▲
THORNTHWAITE CRAG

MILES

0   1   2   3

from Hartsop

NATURAL FEATURES

A lofty ridge, bounded by exceedingly steep flanks, extends northwards from Thornthwaite Crag with a slight curve to the west, and culminates high above Hayeswater Gill in a level platform from which, on both sides, fall precipitous crags split by deep gullies. This is Gray Crag, a prominent object in the Hartsop landscape. Hayeswater forms its eastern base, while the stream issuing therefrom defines it to the north. The western boundary, below an impressive cliff of shattered rocks, is Pasture Beck.

MAP

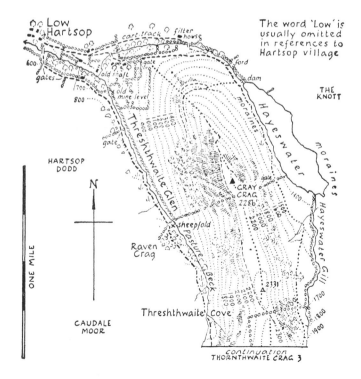

The word 'Low' is usually omitted in references to Hartsop village

continuation
THORNTHWAITE CRAG 3

ASCENT FROM HARTSOP
1800 feet of ascent : 2 miles
(via Threshthwaite Mouth : 1950 feet of ascent : 4 miles)

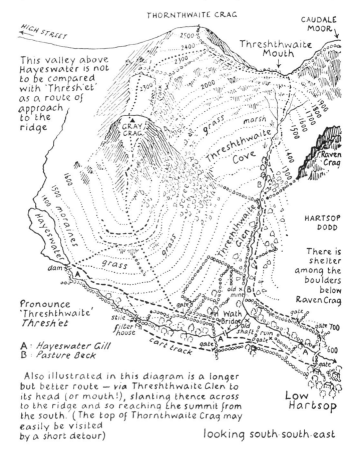

HIGH STREET ←

THORNTHWAITE CRAG

CAUDALE MOOR

Threshthwaite Mouth

This valley above Hayeswater is not to be compared with 'Thresh'et' as a route of approach to the ridge

GRAY CRAG

grass

marsh

Threshthwaite Cove

Raven Crag

moraines

1600

1500

1400

Hayeswater

grass

grass

Threshthwaite Glen

HARTSOP DODD

dam

A

There is shelter among the boulders below Raven Crag

Pronounce 'Threshthwaite' Thresh'et

A : Hayeswater Gill
B : Pasture Beck

stile
filter house
cart track

gate

Wath Bridge
old mine
old shaft
ruin
gate

gate
gate
gate
700
600
gate

Low Hartsop

Also illustrated in this diagram is a longer but better route — via Threshthwaite Glen to its head (or mouth!), slanting thence across to the ridge and so reaching the summit from the south. (The top of Thornthwaite Crag may easily be visited by a short detour)

looking south·south·east

The direct route climbs steeply to the ridge when free of the enclosing walls above Wath Bridge, but it is easier and more interesting to continue first to Hayeswater and gain the ridge from there.

THE SUMMIT

The summit is a pleasant level plateau of grass between steep cliffs, which should be visited for their striking downward views. DESCENTS (to Hartsop): The *only* practicable way off is by the descending north ridge, which narrows and is very enjoyable — the bilberries here are more in evidence as plants than as fruit. *In mist*, keep between the steep slopes (no rock has to be negotiated anywhere) until a plain path is reached *crossing the fellside*, and then another; *beyond these*, avoid a small crag and go down grass slopes to the Hayeswater path above Wath Bridge.

RIDGE ROUTE

To THORNTHWAITE CRAG, 2569'
1¼ miles : slightly E of S
Two minor depressions : 350 feet of ascent
A simple stroll on grass; safe in mist

Sheep tracks may be followed much of the way, but the walking is so easy that they are scarcely worth looking for. The escarpments on both flanks of the ridge are steep enough to warn of danger in mist, when it is necessary to note that *the first two walls are crossed at right angles and the third followed.*

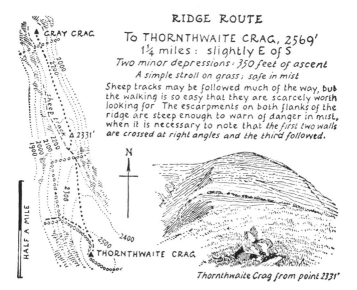

Thornthwaite Crag from point 2331'

THE VIEW

The edges of the escarpments are better viewpoints than the cairn, the steep declivities giving remarkable depth to the scene. While the view from the western edge of the summit is the more extensive, that from the eastern reveals the most striking picture, that of Hayeswater below.

Principal Fells

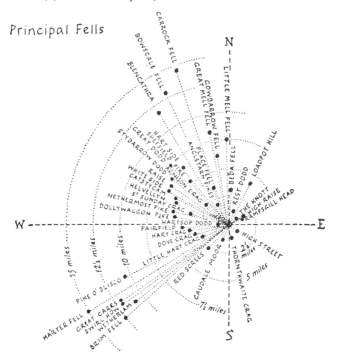

Lakes and Tarns

NNW : *Ullswater* (upper reach)

S : The small sheet of water seen above Threshthwaite Mouth is *Dubbs Reservoir,* Applethwaite Common. *Windermere* can be seen in the same direction by walking 300 yards along the ridge : it is especially well seen from point 2331.

Hayeswater is brought into view by walking 50 yards in the direction of Rampsgill Head from the cairn, *Brothers Water* by walking 80 yards in the direction of Helvellyn.

Cascades above the filter house

Hayeswater Gill

Wath Bridge

Grey Crag

2093'

from Shipman Knotts

▲ HARTER FELL

▲ TARN CRAG

▲ KENTMERE PIKE   ▲ GREY CRAG   ● road summit

Longsleddale ●   Hucks Bridge ●

Jungle Café ●

Garnett Bridge ●   ● Selside

MILES
0 1 2 3 4 5

NATURAL FEATURES

Shap Fells are the high link between the Pennines and Lakeland. They form a broad upland area of smooth grassy slopes and plateaux; inexpressibly wild and desolate but riven by deep valleys having each its lonely sheepfarm; gradually the ground rises in undulating ridges towards a focal point above the head of Longsleddale at the 2000-feet contour. The place of convergence of the ridges is Grey Crag, where is the first evidence, in rocky outcrops and low crags, of the characteristics so peculiar to Lakeland, although the influences of the Pennines persist in the form of peat-hags and marshes. These ridges, on a map, rather resemble the spread fingers and thumb of a hand, with Grey Crag as the palm.

IIIIII 1500'
≣≣≣ 2000'

1 : Grey Crag
2 : Tarn Crag
3 : Capplebarrow
4 : White Howe
5 : Lords Seat
6 : Great Yarlside
7 : Wasdale Pike
8 : Seat Robert
9 : High Wether Howe

A : *Longsleddale*
B : *Bannisdale*
C : *Borrowdale*
D : *Crookdale*
E : *Wasdale*
F : *Wet Sleddale*
G : *Swindale*
H : *Mosedale*

There is nothing remarkable about Grey Crag, but here Lakeland may be said to start and moorland country to end — and the transition is sudden : the quiet beauty gives place to romantic beauty, placid scenery to exciting. One looks east, and the heart is soothed ; west, and it is stirred. Longsleddale, at the western base of the fell, is a lovely valley and, at its head, typically Lakeland. Nearby, across a slight depression north-west, is a twin height, Tarn Crag ; between them is Greycrag Tarn.

Grey Crag 3

MAP

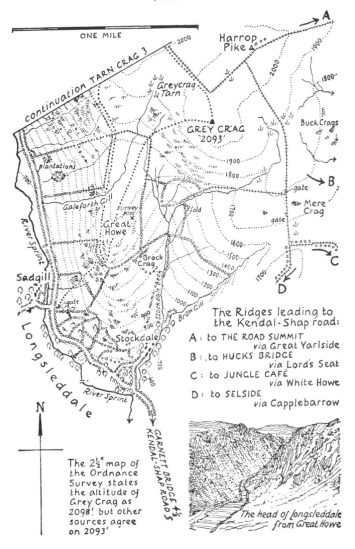

ONE MILE

continuation TARN CRAG 3

A →

Harrop Pike ▲

Greycrag Tarn

GREY CRAG 2093'

Buck Crags

plantations

Galeforth Gill

survey post

Great Howe

fold

gate → B

Mere Crag

gate

River Sprint

Brock Crag

1900
1800
1700
1600
1500
1400
1300
1200
1100
1000
900
800
700

Sadgill

gate

Brow Gill

Stockdale Beck

→ C

D ↓

Stockdale

The Ridges leading to the Kendal-Shap road:

A : to THE ROAD SUMMIT
     via Great Yarlside
B : to HUCKS BRIDGE
     via Lord's Seat
C : to JUNGLE CAFÉ
     via White Howe
D : to SELSIDE
     via Capplebarrow

Longsleddale

River Sprint

N ↑

GARNETT BRIDGE 4½
KENDAL-SHAP ROADS

The 2½" map of the Ordnance Survey states the altitude of Grey Crag as 2098', but other sources agree on 2093'

The head of Longsleddale from Great Howe

ASCENT FROM LONGSLEDDALE
1500 feet of ascent : 1½ miles from Sadgill

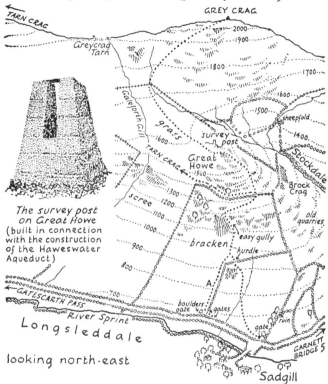

The survey post
on Great Howe
(built in connection
with the construction
of the Haweswater
Aqueduct)

looking north-east

The hurdle across the gap in the wall at the top of the first
enclosure is awkward to negotiate, being too frail to climb.
Ladies, and gentlemen with short legs, will preserve dignity
best by adopting the variation start marked A, so avoiding it.

Great Howe is an excellent viewpoint for Longsleddale.

The ascent should be commenced from Sadgill
Bridge, the more direct Stockdale route being
much less attractive than the climb over Great
Howe. The first thousand feet is steep. In mist,
the ascent has nothing to commend it. No path.

ASCENTS FROM THE KENDAL-SHAP ROAD

Grey Crag may be approached from the eastern fringe of the district along any of four clearly-defined ridges each of which has independent and distinct summits — and all of which descend to the main Kendal-Shap road. These approaches are described on this and the opposite page

1: from   SELSIDE   and   JUNGLE CAFÉ

1700 feet of ascent   1650 feet of ascent
7 miles   6 miles

GREY CRAG

Harrop Pike

Great Yarlside

Crookdale

Mere Crag

Lords Seat

grass

foundation of old wall alongside fence

heather

Long Crag

Survey column

These are the two ridges featured on the opposite page

tarn

Bannisdale Head

White Howe

This Borrowdale is not to be confused with its famous Cumberland namesake

continuous fence to Harrop Pike

grass

Borrowdale

Capplebarrow
Excellent viewpoint

grass

shooting butts

heather

heathery hummocks

Nab End

stiles

heather

hut

The circuit of Bannisdale by the ridges is itself an excellent walk. The best way round is clockwise, ascending via Capplebarrow and descending via White Howe.

gate

Whiteside Pike 1302'
— a delectable summit of rock and heather. Excellent views.

Jungle Café

tarn

fields

Bannisdale is concealed from the main road by a screen of trees and low hills.

SHAP 8

Moser (farm)

BANNISDALE

Plough Inn
an inspired inn-sign!

MAIN ROAD

looking north-north-west

KENDAL 5

Selside

Refer to the notes at the foot of the opposite page

ASCENTS FROM THE KENDAL-SHAP ROAD

2 : from HUCKS BRIDGE and **THE ROAD SUMMIT**
1700 feet of ascent   1000 feet of ascent
5 miles   5 miles

looking west·north·west

GREY CRAG   Harrop Pike   Great Yarlside 1900   Wasdale Pike

Mere Crag   1800   Buck Crags   Yarlside Crag   1800   1700

Red Crag   1700   Blaeberry Gill   1700   1600   × sheepfold (ruins)   1600   1500   Little Yarlside

Lord's Seat   1600 beacon   Robin Hood   Crookdale   1500   Wasdale (the Westmorland Wasdale)

Borrowdale (the Westmorland Borrowdale)

gate   gate   1500 beacon 1600   High House Bank   1500 1400 ×1300   1200   1100   1000   Watshaw Common   1500

1400   pylon   kiosk   SHAP 5½

Ask permission to cross this field if the farmer is watching.

JUNGLE CAFÉ 1   High Borrow Bridge   gate   old road   MAIN ROAD   ✱Eagles Nest Café   road summit

KENDAL 8½   900   gate   Hucks Bridge   ✱ STOP PRESS: The proprietors of the Eagle Nest Café have recently changed its name to Fell Top Café.

The Yarlside ridge is the easier of the two illustrated; moreover, its continuous fence makes it safe in mist

It should be noted particularly that these routes lie across very lonely territory, in striking contrast to the pulsating life and movement of the unceasing traffic on the slender ribbon of road; there are no paths along the ridges, and visitors are infrequent. The desolation is profound. Solitary walkers who want a decent burial should bear in mind that if an accident befalls them in this wilderness their bones are likely to adorn the scene until they rot and disintegrate.

These walks are more Pennine than Lakeland in character: there is very little rock but much tough grass and heather, and peat-hags and marshes are unwelcome features. Because of the nature of the ground, the traverse of the ridges should be undertaken only after a period of dry weather; they are best left alone on a wet day or during a rainy season or if under snow. Subject to the disabilities mentioned, it may be stated at once that the ridges offer easy and exhilarating walking in impressive surroundings, while the wide horizons and the vast skyscapes deserve the brush of a Turner.

This is fine open country, but it is not Lakeland.

THE SUMMIT

The top of the fell is extensive, but the highest point, indicated by a cairn, is not in doubt although it stands but little above a wide expanse of small outcrops and peat-hags.

DESCENTS: In clear weather, with ample time in hand, a way may be made to the Kendal-Shap road by any of the four ridges. If Longsleddale is the objective, the descent should be made by Great Howe in preference to a direct route via Stockdale.

In bad conditions, the descent to the Kendal-Shap road must not be undertaken lightly. Note that only the Yarlside ridge has a continuous fence or wall all the way to the road. For Longsleddale, *in mist*, pick a way straight down into Stockdale to avoid the scarps on Great Howe.

The cairn on Harrop Pike

Mere Crag

— a remarkably 'clean' face of rock, showing no sign of decay, lush grass grows up to its base. Climbers will enjoy its slabs.

RIDGE ROUTE
TO TARN CRAG, 2176'
¾ mile : N then NW and SSW
Depression at 1940:
250 feet of ascent

Straightforward walking, but it is better to skirt the marshes of Greycrag Tarn by keeping along the side of the fence.

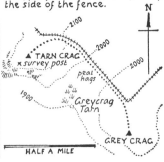

N

2100
2000
2000

▲ TARN CRAG
× survey post

peat hags

1900

Greycrag Tarn

GREY CRAG ▲

HALF A MILE

THE VIEW

Grey Crag is the most easterly of the Lakeland fells, but is not of sufficient elevation to provide the panorama across the district that might be expected from its position. Higher neighbours around the head of Longsleddale conceal most of the better-known mountains, but the Coniston group is quite prominent and there is a peep of the Scafells over the saddle between Yoke and Ill Bell.

Principal Fells

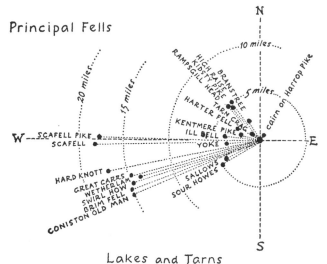

Lakes and Tarns

SSW: Skeggles Water
SW: Windermere (two sections)

Although the view towards Lakeland is disappointingly restricted, there can be no complaint of the quality of the prospects in other directions. On a clear day the panorama is remarkably extensive and very beautiful; there is a vastness, a spaciousness, about it that is usually lacking in the views from Lakeland summits. Just to the right of the cairn on Harrop Pike, Cross Fell and the twin Dun Fells start a glorious sweep of the Pennines extending south as far as Pendle Hill, with the principal heights of Mickle Fell, the Mallerstang fells, Whernside and Ingleborough all prominent. The nearer Howgill Fells, which always look attractive, are excellently grouped. Southwards is Kendal and the Kent Valley, and, beyond, Morecambe Bay silvers the horizon round to the isolated mass of Black Combe. There can be few better views in the country—but the days on which it is fully visible are also few, unfortunately.

Hallin Fell

from above Mellguards

Hallin Fell, beautifully situated overlooking a curve of Ullswater and commanding unrivalled views of the lovely secluded hinterland of Martindale, may be regarded as the motorists' fell, for the sandals and slippers and polished shoes of the numerous car-owners who park their properties on the crest of the road above the Howtown zig-zags on Sunday afternoons have smoothed to its summit a wide track that is seldom violated by the hobnails of fellwalkers. In choosing Hallin Fell as their weekend picnic-place and playground the Penrith and Carlisle motorists show commendable discrimination, for the rich rewards its summit offers are out of all proportion to the slight effort of ascent.

HALLIN FELL
● ▲ ●
Sandwick   Howtown

PLACE ▲   ▲ BEDA
FELL   FELL

● Patterdale

MILES
0   1   2   3

MAP

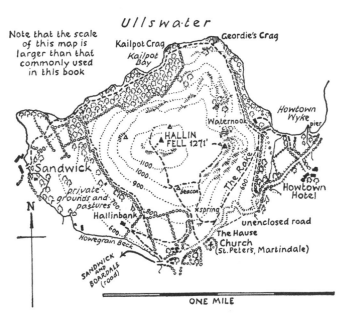

Ullswater

Note that the scale of this map is larger than that commonly used in this book

Kailpot Crag

Geordie's Crag

Kailpot Bay

Howtown Wyke

pier

Waternook

HALLIN FELL 1271'

Sandwick

The Race

Howtown Hotel

private grounds and pastures

beacon

x spring

Hallinbank

unenclosed road

Howegrain Beck

The Hause Church (St. Peters, Martindale)

SANDWICK AND BOARDALE (road)

ONE MILE

ASCENTS

There is one royal road to the top: this is the wide grass path leaving the Hause opposite the church, and it can be ascended comfortably in bare feet; in dry weather the short smooth turf is slippery. Another track from the Hause visits the large cairn overlooking Howtown, and offers an alternative route to the top! Incidentally (although this has nothing to do with *fell*-walking!) the lakeside path *via* Kailpot Crag is entirely delightful.

HIGH RAISE · RAMPSGILL HEAD · THE KNOTT · REST DODD · GRAY CRAG · CAUDALE MOOR · LITTLE HART CRAG · DOVE CRAG

THE NAB · BEDA FELL · ANGLETARN PIKES

The Martindale skyline, from the top of Hallin Fell

THE SUMMIT

'The man who built the summit-cairn of Hallin Fell did more than indicate the highest point : he erected for himself a permanent memorial. This 12-foot obelisk, a landmark for miles around, is a massive structure of squared and prepared stone. The undulating top of the fell suffers from a rash of smaller, insignificant cairns : they occupy not merely the many vantage-points but even the bottoms of sundry hollows.
The top is mainly grassy with bracken encroaching; there is a good deal of outcropping rock.

DESCENTS : The temptation to descend east directly to Howtown should be resisted for the slope above the Rake is rough and unpleasant.
The easiest way off, and the quickest, is by the path going down to the church on the Hause. *In mist,* no other route can safely be attempted.

The lower reach of Ullswater from the north cairn

THE VIEW

Principal Fells

The bird's-eye view of Ullswater is dramatic, but the classic scene unfolded is an intimate one of green fields and steep fells, the Martindale district, for which this is the best viewpoint. The panorama is good considering the modest elevation.

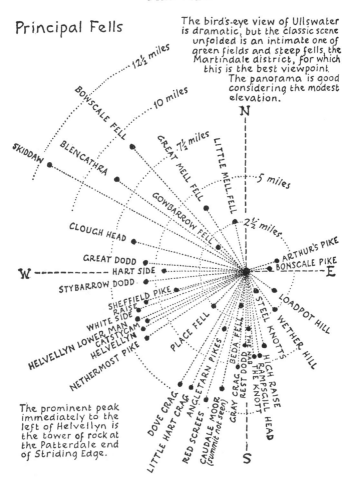

The prominent peak immediately to the left of Helvellyn is the tower of rock at the Patterdale end of Striding Edge.

Lakes and Tarns

WSW to NE : *Ullswater*
(all of the middle and lower reaches)

Harter Fell

2539'

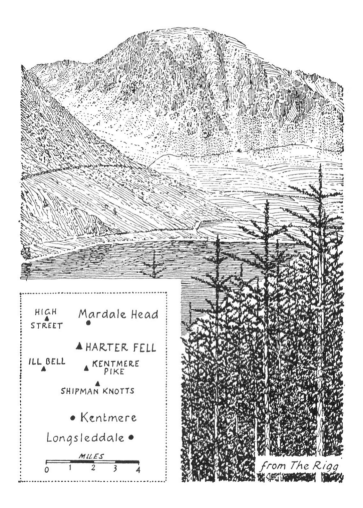

HIGH
STREET

Mardale Head ●

▲ HARTER FELL

ILL BELL
▲

▲ KENTMERE
PIKE

▲ SHIPMAN KNOTTS

● Kentmere

Longsleddale ●

MILES

0   1   2   3   4

from The Rigg

NATURAL FEATURES

A broad wedge of lonely upland country rises from the valley of the Kent at Burneside and continues north, narrowing, between the valleys of Kentmere and Longsleddale for nine miles; until, having very gradually attained its maximum height on Harter Fell, the ground suddenly collapses in a tremendous wall of crags, falling swiftly to the head of Mardale amongst wild and romantic surroundings — one of the noblest mountain scenes in the district. This northern face is Harter Fell's chief glory, for here, too, a shelf cradles Small Water, which is the finest of Lakeland's tarns in the opinion of many qualified to judge: seen in storm, the picture is most impressive and awe-inspiring. The other slopes have less of note although Drygrove Gill is an interesting example of landslip and Wren Gill has extensive (and dangerous) quarries. Harter Fell is one of the few fells that can claim a well-known pass on either side of its summit: Nan Bield Pass on the west and Gatescarth Pass on the east link Kentmere and Longsleddale respectively with Mardale, but since the hamlet of Mardale Head was 'drowned' by Haweswater (shame!) these passes have largely fallen from favour.

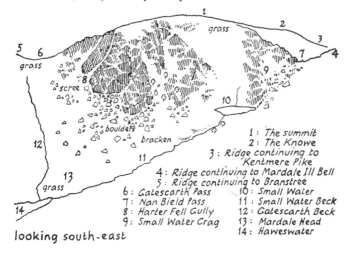

1: The summit
2: The Knowe
3: Ridge continuing to Kentmere Pike
4: Ridge continuing to Mardale Ill Bell
5: Ridge continuing to Branstree
6: Gatescarth Pass
7: Nan Bield Pass
8: Harter Fell Gully
9: Small Water Crag
10: Small Water
11: Small Water Beck
12: Gatescarth Beck
13: Mardale Head
14: Haweswater

looking south-east

MAP

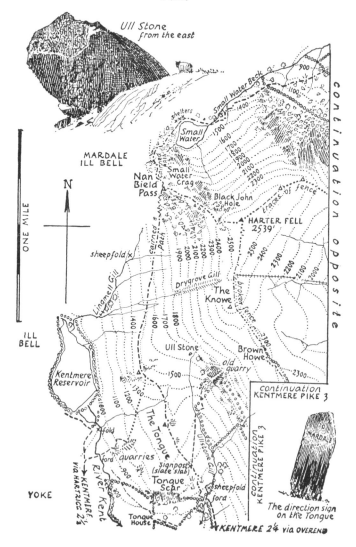

Ull Stone from the east

continuation opposite

ONE MILE

MARDALE ILL BELL

N

ILL BELL

YOKE

900

Small Water Beck

shelters

Small Water

Nan Bield Pass

Small Water Crag

Black John Hole

traces of fence

HARTER FELL 2539'

sheepfold ×

Lingmell Gill

cairned path

Drygrove Gill

The Knowe

broken fence

Ull Stone

Brown Howe

old quarry

Kentmere Reservoir

fold

ford

quarries

The Tongue

signpost (slate slab)

Tongue Scar

sheepfold

ford

Ullstone Gill

KENTMERE 2¼ via HARTRIGG

River Kent

Tongue House

KENTMERE 2¼ via OVEREND

continuation KENTMERE PIKE 3

continuation KENTMERE PIKE 3

MARDALE

The direction sign on the Tongue

MAP

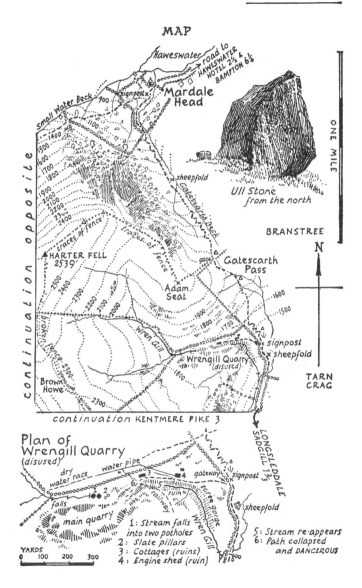

Haweswater

road to
HAWESWATER
HOTEL 2½ &
BAMPTON 6¼

signpost

Mardale Head

Small Water Beck

900

ONE MILE

Ull Stone
from the north

sheepfold

BRANSTREE

N

HARTER FELL
2539'

traces of fence

gate

Gatescarth Pass

Adam Seat

1600

1500

broken fence

Wren Gill

signpost
sheepfold

Wrengill Quarry
(disused)

Brown Howe

TARN CRAG

continuation opposite

continuation KENTMERE PIKE 3

LONGSLEDDALE SADGILL 1⅓

Plan of Wrengill Quarry
(disused)

dry water race

water pipe

railway

gateway

signpost

falls

main quarry

Wren Gill

gorge

sheepfold

1: Stream falls
into two potholes
2: Slate pillars
3: Cottages (ruins)
4: Engine shed (ruin)

5: Stream re-appears
6: Path collapsed
and DANGEROUS

YARDS
0   100   200   300

The west face of Harter Fell
from the north-east ridge of Ill Bell

ASCENT FROM KENTMERE
2200 feet of ascent
5¼ miles via Nan Bield Pass :   4¼ miles via Kentmere Pike

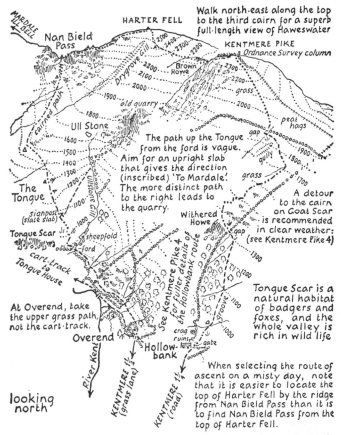

MARDALE ILL BELL

Nan Bield Pass

HARTER FELL

Walk north-east along the top to the third cairn for a superb full-length view of Haweswater

KENTMERE PIKE   Ordnance Survey column

Dry grove Gill

2500 2400 2300 2200

Brown Howe

2300 2200

2200

2000

grass

old quarry

1900

2000

1800

Ull Stone

peat hags

1600

1500

1400

1300

The Tongue

1200

1100

Ullstone Gill

The path up the Tongue from the ford is vague. Aim for an upright slab that gives the direction (inscribed) 'To Mardale'. The more distinct path to the right leads to the quarry.

gap

gully

1900 1800

1700

grass

A detour to the cairn on Goat Scar is recommended in clear weather: (see Kentmere Pike 4)

signpost (slate slab)

1000

Tongue Scar

sheepfold

ford

cart-track to Tongue House

Withered Howe

gap

1300

Tongue Scar is a natural habitat of badgers and foxes, and the whole valley is rich in wild life

At Overend, take the upper grass path, not the cart-track.

Overend

See Kentmere Pike 4 for fuller details of the Hollowbank route

groove

1100

1000

crag ruins

Hollow-bank

gate

River Kent

KENTMERE 1½ (grass lane)

KENTMERE 1½ (road)

When selecting the route of ascent on a misty day, note that it is easier to locate the top of Harter Fell by the ridge from Nan Bield Pass than it is to find Nan Bield Pass from the top of Harter Fell.

looking north

Two routes are shown. That from Hollowbank is both easier and shorter, that from Overend much the more beautiful and interesting. The round journey serves as an excellent introduction to upper Kentmere. The sharp-crested Nan Bield is the finest of Lakeland passes.

ASCENT FROM LONGSLEDDALE
1950 feet of ascent : 4¼ miles from Sadgill

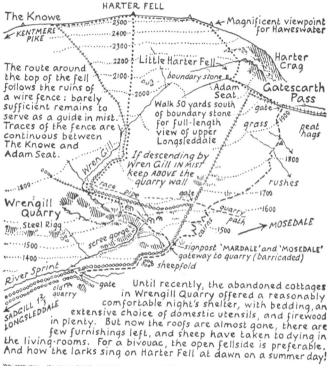

HARTER FELL

The Knowe

Magnificent viewpoint for Haweswater

KENTMERE PIKE

2500
2400
2300
2200 Little Harter Fell
2100 boundary stone

Harter Crag

Gatescarth Pass

2000

Adam Seat

gate

peat hags

The route around the top of the fell follows the ruins of a wire fence : barely sufficient remains to serve as a guide in mist. Traces of the fence are continuous between The Knowe and Adam Seat.

Walk 50 yards south of boundary stone for full-length view of upper Longsleddale

grass

If descending by Wren Gill IN MIST keep ABOVE the quarry wall

1800

1800

rushes

Wren Gill

race pipe

gate

1700

Wrengill Quarry

Steel Rigg

quarry path

cairns

1600

MOSEDALE

1500

scree gorge

signpost 'MARDALE' and 'MOSEDALE' gateway to quarry (barricaded)

1500
1400

sheepfold

River Sprint

old quarry

gate

SADGILL 1⅔ LONGSLEDDALE

Until recently, the abandoned cottages in Wrengill Quarry offered a reasonably comfortable night's shelter, with bedding, an extensive choice of domestic utensils, and firewood in plenty. But now the roofs are almost gone, there are few furnishings left, and sheep have taken to dying in the living-rooms. For a bivouac, the open fellside is preferable. And how the larks sing on Harter Fell at dawn on a summer day!

The disappearance of Wren Gill

looking north-west

The Gatescarth route is particularly easy: a hands-in-pockets stroll with no steep climbing, the top being reached with surprising lack of effort. Nonagenarians will find it eminently suitable.
Avoid Wren Gill in mist.

ASCENT FROM MARDALE
1750 feet of ascent : 2 miles from the road end

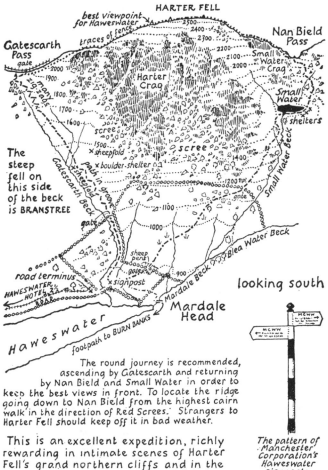

HARTER FELL

best viewpoint for Haweswater

traces of fence

2500
2400
2300
2200
2100
2000

Nan Bield Pass

Gatescarth Pass
gate

Small Water Crag

Harter Crag

Small Water

zigzags

2000
1900
1800
1700
1600

shelters

scree
1500
× sheepfold
× boulder-shelter
scree

1400
1300

The steep fell on this side of the beck is BRANSTREE

Gatescarth Beck

path in groove

× sheepfold
gate

1200

gate

Small Water Beck

1100
1000

sheep pens
gate
× signpost

900

Blea Water Beck

Mardale Beck

looking south

road terminus
HAWESWATER HOTEL 3⁄4

Mardale Head

Haweswater

footpath to BURN BANKS

The round journey is recommended, ascending by Gatescarth and returning by Nan Bield and Small Water in order to keep the best views in front. To locate the ridge going down to Nan Bield from the highest cairn walk in the direction of Red Screes. Strangers to Harter Fell should keep off it in bad weather.

This is an excellent expedition, richly rewarding in intimate scenes of Harter Fell's grand northern cliffs and in the views of Haweswater from its summit, yet short in distance and needing much less effort in execution than its formidable appearance suggests.

The pattern of Manchester Corporation's Haweswater signposts

THE SUMMIT

A mild shock awaits anyone reaching the top of the fell on a first visit, especially in mist, for there is a spectral weirdness about the two highest cairns. The stones support an elaborate superstructure of iron fence-posts and railings, which, having served their original mission, now act as an adornment that has a nightmarish quality.

The highest part of the fell, a graceful curve, is a long grassy sheep-walk. The fence that formerly traversed its length is now in complete ruin, but can still be traced, and is followed by the pedestrian route across the top. As so often on easy ground, no paths have been trodden out, and only occasionally does a faint track materialise.

The altitude of Harter Fell is variously stated by different authorities as 2509', 2539', 2560' and 2585'. The Ordnance Survey figure of 2539' is reliable.

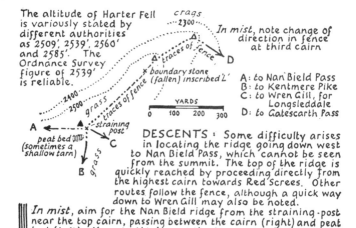

In mist, note change of direction in fence at third cairn

A: to Nan Bield Pass
B: to Kentmere Pike
C: to Wren Gill, for Longsleddale
D: to Gatescarth Pass

DESCENTS: Some difficulty arises in locating the ridge going down west to Nan Bield Pass, which cannot be seen from the summit. The top of the ridge is quickly reached by proceeding directly from the highest cairn towards Red Screes. Other routes follow the fence, although a quick way down to Wren Gill may also be noted.

||| *In mist*, aim for the Nan Bield ridge from the straining-post near the top cairn, passing between the cairn (right) and peat bed (left). Keep to the line of the fence on other routes.

Haweswater
from the third cairn

THE VIEW

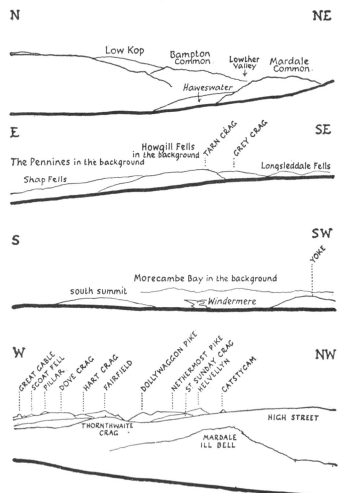

N   **NE**

Low Kop   Bampton Common   Lowther Valley   Mardale Common

Haweswater

E   **SE**

Howgill Fells in the background   TARN CRAG   GREY CRAG

The Pennines in the background

Shap Fells   Longsleddale Fells

S   **SW**

YOKE

Morecambe Bay in the background

south summit   Windermere

W   **NW**

GREAT GABLE   SCOAT FELL   PILLAR   DOVE CRAG   HART CRAG   FAIRFIELD   DOLLYWAGGON PIKE   NETHERMOST PIKE   ST SUNDAY CRAG   HELVELLYN   CATSTYCAM

THORNTHWAITE CRAG

HIGH STREET

MARDALE ILL BELL

THE VIEW

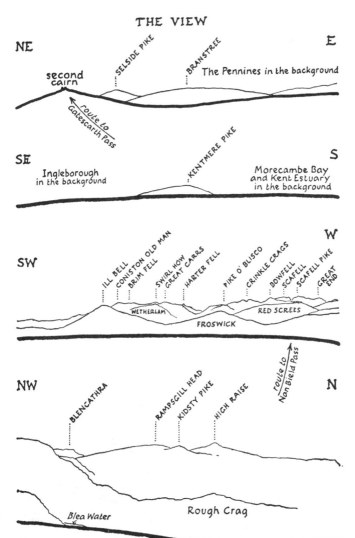

NE

second cairn

SELSIDE PIKE

BRANSTREE

The Pennines in the background

E

route to Gatescarth Pass

SE

Ingleborough in the background

KENTMERE PIKE

Morecambe Bay and Kent Estuary in the background

S

SW

ILL BELL
CONISTON OLD MAN
BRIM FELL
SWIRL HOW
GREAT CARRS
HARTER FELL
PIKE O' BLISCO
CRINKLE CRAGS
BOWFELL
SCAFELL
SCAFELL PIKE
GREAT END

WETHERLAM

RED SCREES

FROSWICK

W

NW

BLENCATHRA

RAMPSGILL HEAD
KIDSTY PIKE
HIGH RAISE

route to Nan Bield Pass

N

Blea Water

Rough Crag

Blea Water cannot be seen from the cairn, but is brought into view by walking a few yards north-west.

RIDGE ROUTES

To BRANSTREE, 2333': 2 miles: NE then SE and NE
Depression at 1875'(Gatescarth Pass) : 465 feet of ascent
An easy walk on grass, tedious beyond Gatescarth

Follow the line of the old fence around the watershed to the good fence on Adam Seat: this runs unbroken across Gatescarth Pass and up to the top of Branstree. *In mist, it is important to note the sharp angle in the route at the third cairn: crags are ahead.*

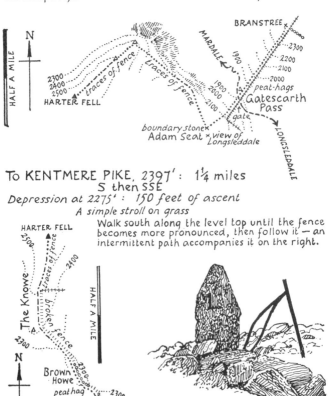

To KENTMERE PIKE, 2397': 1¼ miles
S then SSE
Depression at 2275' : 150 feet of ascent
A simple stroll on grass

Walk south along the level top until the fence becomes more pronounced, then follow it — an intermittent path accompanies it on the right.

Boundary stone on Adam Seat

RIDGE ROUTE

To MARDALE ILL BELL, 2496': W, then WNW and NW
1 mile

Depression at 2100' (Nan Bield Pass) :   450 feet of ascent

An excellent crossing of a fine pass, with beautiful and impressive views
Aim west (in the direction of Red Screes) until the ridge going down to Nan Bield is seen below: this is a delectable descent, Small Water being a striking feature. Nan Bield is marked by a big cairn-shelter; round the outcrop beyond on the left side. Slant up to the right over rough ground when the path fades and watch for the white boulders that indicate the final rise to the summit. *In mist, Mardale Ill Bell is confusing and dangerous ; there are no paths across the top.*

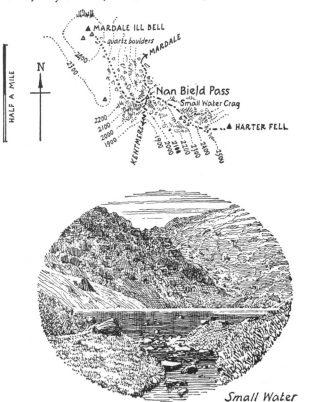

Small Water

Hartsop Dodd

2018'

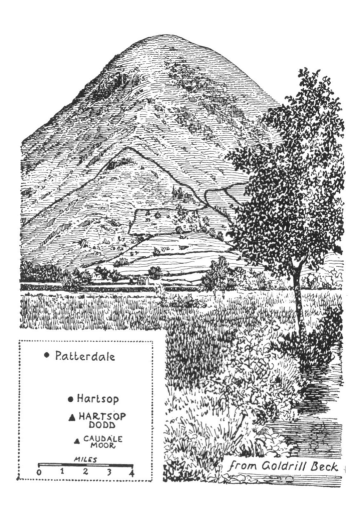

Patterdale

Hartsop

▲ HARTSOP
DODD

▲ CAUDALE
MOOR

MILES

0   1   2   3   4

from Goldrill Beck

NATURAL FEATURES

For a few miles along the road from Patterdale to Kirkstone, Hartsop Dodd has the form of a steepsided conical hill, rising like a giant tumulus from the flat floor of the valley; a high ridge connecting with the loftier Caudale Moor behind is unseen and unsuspected. After the fashion of many subsidiary fells in this area, the imposing front is a sham, for the Dodd is no more than the knuckled fist at the end of one of the several arms of Caudale Moor. It rises from pleasant places, pastures and woods and water, and quite rightly has been named from the delightful hamlet nestling unspoilt among trees at its foot.

It is interesting to note that Hartsop Dodd (*Low* Hartsop Dodd) has a greater elevation than its counterpart *High* Hartsop Dodd nearby, the prefixes relating to their geographical positions in the valley, not to their altitudes

The word 'Low' is usually omitted in references to Hartsop village

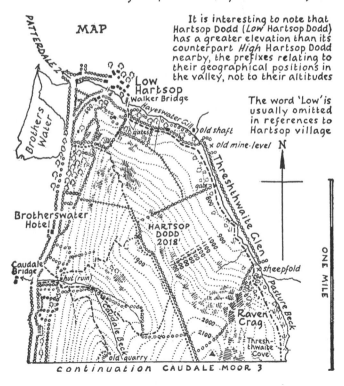

MAP

PATTERDALE 2

Low Hartsop

Walker Bridge

Hayeswater Gill

Brothers Water

gates

old shaft

× old mine level

N

Threshthwaite Glen

gate

Brotherswater Hotel

HARTSOP DODD 2018'

900

Caudale Bridge

hut (ruin)

1900

800

1000

1100

1200

1300

sheepfold

Pasture Beck

ONE MILE

Caudale Beck

2000

Raven Crag

Threshthwaite Cove

2100

old quarry

continuation CAUDALE MOOR 3

ASCENTS

A feature of the paths leading up Hartsop Dodd is that, for much of their length, they run in well-engineered grooves that help considerably in defining the routes. The best way up is by the steep north ridge, a beautiful climb. The path zigzagging up the west flank is also steep, and rather dreary. The only easy route follows Caudale Beck at first and ultimately gains the ridge between the Dodd and Caudale Moor; this way is dull.

THE SUMMIT

A wall crosses the grassy top, the highest point being indicated by a wooden fence-post against the wall from which a fence formerly went down the fellside. A few stones fallen from the wall at its first bend southwards have been piled together to form a cairn of no significance.

High Raise   Rampsgill Head   Gray Crag   The Knott

RIDGE ROUTE

HARTSOP DODD

Raven Crag

Threshthwaite Cove

ONE MILE

N

1900, 1800, 1500, 1800, 1900, 2000, 2100, 2200, 2300, 2400

CAUDALE MOOR

DESCENTS: The grooves do not continue onto the summit. To find the path going down to the west, walk in the direction of Dove Crag, passing by two more fence-posts minus fence — the top of the groove is just beyond the second. To find the path down the north ridge walk towards Ullswater — the groove starts soon after the ground steepens; keep to the ridge and avoid the parallel gully on the right. The longer easy route is scarcely worth consideration.

In mist, the path on the west will be easiest to find — leave the top fence-post at right angles to the wall and look for the other two which give the key to the descent.

To CAUDALE MOOR, 2502'
1½ miles : SSE, then S
Depression at 1900': 620 feet of ascent

An easy climb on grass, safe in mist. The wall drearily links the two summits. In fine weather, interest may be introduced into the walk by following the edge of the escarpment on the left, the views therefrom down into Threshthwaite being very striking.

THE VIEW

The view of Dove Crag and Dovedale across the gulf of the Patterdale valley is exceedingly impressive, a classic amongst views. Red Screes, too, rises majestically and steeply from the depths of Kirkstone. The edges of the summit, rather than the top, give the best views.

Principal Fells

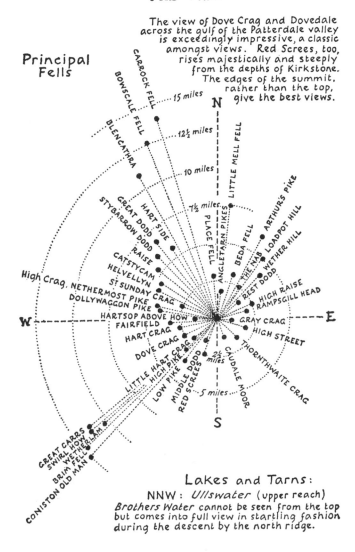

Lakes and Tarns:
NNW: *Ullswater* (upper reach)
Brothers Water cannot be seen from the top but comes into full view in startling fashion during the descent by the north ridge.

Dovedale

Patterdale

- Howtown
- Martindale
    Bampton •
  ▲ WETHER HILL
    Measand
  ▲ HIGH RAISE
  ▲ • Riggindale
  HIGH STREET

MILES
0   1   2   3   4

*from the col
below The Knott*

NATURAL FEATURES

Second in altitude among the fells east of Kirkstone and Ullswater, High Raise is overtopped only by High Street itself. Topographically, it cannot be said to occupy an important position, for it commands no valleys and it is not a meeting-place of ridges; yet, nevertheless, its summit-cone rises distinctively from the lofty watershed of the main range, and it is the last fell, going north, with the characteristics of a mountain — beyond are rolling foothills. Flanking it on the west is the valley of Rampsgill, to which falls abruptly a featureless wall of grass and scree. Much more extensive, and much more interesting, are the eastern declivities, going down to Haweswater: here natural forces have scooped out a great hollow just below the subsidiary summit of Low Raise, leaving a mile-long fringe of crags between two airy ridges.

There are considerable streams on this flank, and all flow into Haweswater. Formerly these waters helped to irrigate the fertile Lowther and Eden valleys, but nowadays only the most favoured do so: the fate of the majority is captive travel along less pleasurable routes to the taps of Manchester, there to serve the needs of man in other ways.

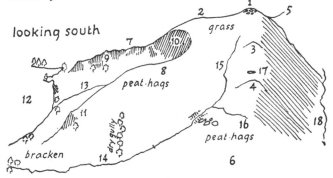

looking south

1 : The summit	2 : Low Raise	3 : Raven Howe	4 : Red Crag
5 : Ridge continuing to Rampsgill Head	6 : Ridge continuing to Wether Hill
7 : South-east ridge	8 : North-east ridge	9 : Birks Crag
10 : Whelter Crags	11 : Lad Crags	12 :
13 : Whelter Beck	14 : Measand Beck	15 : Longgrain Beck
16 : Keasgill Head	17 : Redcrag Tarn	18 : Rampsgill Beck

1 : The summit   2 : Low Raise   3 : Raven Howe 4 : Red Crag
5 : Ridge continuing to Rampsgill Head 6 : Ridge continuing to Wether Hill
7 : South-east ridge 8 : North-east ridge 9 : Birks Crag
10 : Whelter Crags 11 : Lad Crags 12 :
13 : Whelter Beck 14 : Measand Beck 15 : Longgrain Beck
16 : Keasgill Head 17 : Redcrag Tarn 18 : Rampsgill Beck

MAP

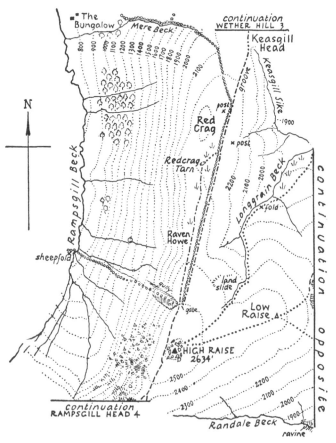

Rampsgill is within the Martindale Deer Forest.
There are no public paths in this valley.

ONE MILE

MAP

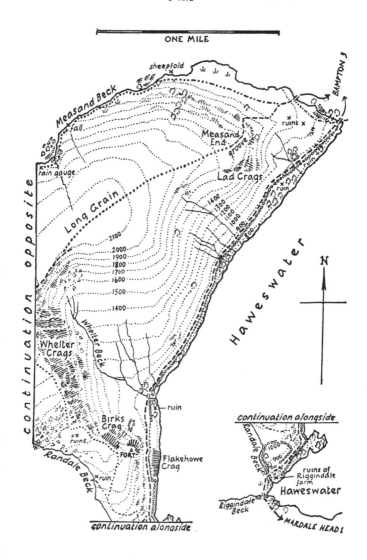

ONE MILE

ASCENTS FROM PATTERDALE AND HARTSOP
2400 feet of ascent : 5¼ miles from Patterdale
2250 feet of ascent : 3½ miles from Hartsop

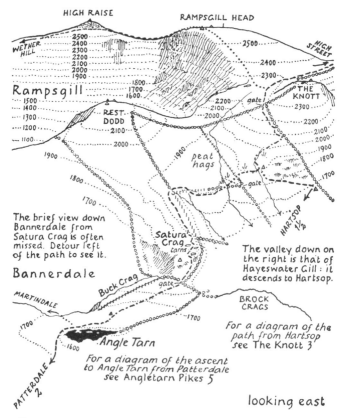

HIGH RAISE

RAMPSGILL HEAD

WETHER HILL

HIGH STREET

2500
2400
2300
2200
2100
2000
1900

2500

2400

2300

Rampsgill

1800
1700
1600

THE KNOTT

1500
1400
1300
1200
1100

REST DODD
2100

2200
2100
2000

2300

2200
2100
2000
1900
1800
1700

1900

2000

1900

peat hags

gate

gate

HARTSOP ½

1800

1700

The brief view down
Bannerdale from
Satura Crag is often
missed. Detour left
of the path to see it.

Satura Crag
tarns

The valley down on
the right is that of
Hayeswater Gill : it
descends to Hartsop.

Bannerdale

Buck Crag

gate

MARTINDALE

BROCK CRAGS

1700

1700

For a diagram of the
path from Hartsop
see The Knott 3

1600

Angle Tarn

PATTERDALE 2

For a diagram of the ascent
to Angle Tarn from Patterdale
see Angletarn Pikes 5

looking east

This is a most enjoyable excursion with a succession
of widely differing views, all excellent; and the route
itself, never very distinct, is an interesting puzzle to
unravel. In bad weather, however, there will be some
difficulty, and a stranger may run into trouble on top
of Rampsgill Head, where there are crags.

ASCENT FROM MARTINDALE
2100 feet of ascent : 5 miles from Martindale (Old Church)

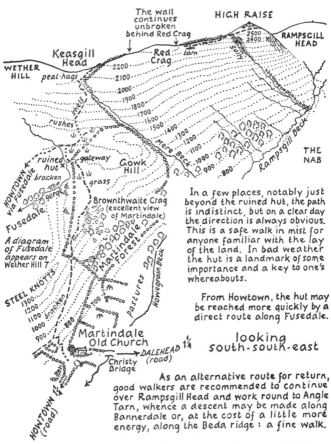

The wall continues unbroken behind Red Crag

HIGH RAISE

2500
2400

RAMPSGILL HEAD

Keasgill Head

Red Crag

tarn

WETHER HILL

peat hags

2200
2100
2000
1900
1800
1700
1600
1500
1400
1300
1200
1100
1000
900
800

shelf

rushes

Mere Beck

Rampsgill Beck

THE NAB

ruined hut

gateway

Gowk Hill

grass

bracken

HOWTOWN via Fusedale

gorge

Fusedale

Brownthwaite Crag (excellent view of Martindale)

A diagram of Fusedale appears on Wether Hill 7

Martindale Forest

Howegrain Beck

STEEL KNOTTS

1300
1200
1100
1000
900

bracken

pastures

Martindale Old Church

DALEHEAD (road) ¼

Christy Bridge

HOWTOWN (road) ¼

In a few places, notably just beyond the ruined hut, the path is indistinct, but on a clear day the direction is always obvious. This is a safe walk in mist for anyone familiar with the lay of the land. In bad weather the hut is a landmark of some importance and a key to one's whereabouts.

From Howtown, the hut may be reached more quickly by a direct route along Fusedale.

looking south-south-east

As an alternative route for return, good walkers are recommended to continue over Rampsgill Head and work round to Angle Tarn, whence a descent may be made along Bannerdale or, at the cost of a little more energy, along the Beda ridge : a fine walk.

This is the only full-size mountain expedition conveniently available from the neighbourhood of Martindale and Howtown. It hardly lives up to its early promise, the middle section being dull, but the views are excellent throughout.

ASCENTS FROM MARDALE
1900 feet of ascent
2½ miles from Riggindale ; 3½ miles from Measand

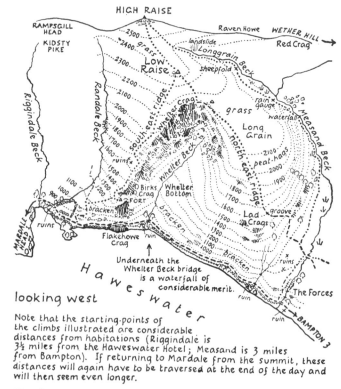

looking west

Note that the starting-points of
the climbs illustrated are considerable
distances from habitations (Riggindale is
3½ miles from the Haweswater Hotel ; Measand is 3 miles
from Bampton). If returning to Mardale from the summit, these
distances will again have to be traversed at the end of the day and
will then seem even longer.

The zig-zag path at the foot of the south-east ridge went out of use
when the nearby buildings were submerged, and is now difficult to
find and follow. All who ascend by this route are recommended to
make a small detour to visit the remains of the ancient fort, which,
crag-defended and double-moated, occupied a striking position, and
even today its ruins are a stimulus to the imagination.

The routes depicted are unfrequented and without
paths except initially. All are interesting, and the
south-east ridge especially is an attractive climb.

*Haweswater, from Measand
at the foot of the north-east ridge*

*The British Fort
on the south-east ridge
with Haweswater beyond*

THE SUMMIT

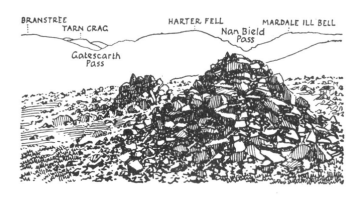

The true fell-walker appreciates best a summit with rocks; failing that, a summit with stones. He will, therefore, have an affectionate regard for High Raise, especially if his visit follows a tour of the neighbouring fells, for its top is crowned with stones in a quantity uncommon amongst the heights of the High Street range, which are usually grassy — they are rough, weathered and colourful stones, a pleasure to behold. Some have been used in the erection of a large cairn; others form an effective wind shelter alongside. The old High Street, here merely a narrow track, crosses the top below the cap of stones, 100 yards west of the cairn. It is the only path.

A long half-mile away, slightly north of east, is the rounded hump of Low Raise. Here all is grass except for a remarkable oasis of bleached stones, obviously transported — a tumulus. These stones were a convenient quarry for later generations whose preference it was to build cairns rather than tumuli, and a really handsome edifice has been constructed.

The tumulus and cairn on Low Raise

DESCENTS

Since the friendly inn and farmsteads of Mardale were so cruelly sacrificed for the common good (sic), the summit of High Raise has been remote from tourist accommodation. It should be noted that the only beds in Mardale nowadays are concentrated in the new Haweswater Hotel, which, for walkers, is sited on the wrong side of the lake, and which, unlike the old Dun Bull, is much more a motorists' resort than a refuge for foot-travellers and shepherds.

Ample time should be allowed for descents, which are lengthy in all directions, and confusing in all directions except to the east, especially so in bad weather.

The natural inclination to scramble down into Rampsgill must be resisted: this valley offers sanctuary for deer, and there is neither welcome nor lodging for two-legged animals.

Descents should not be made in the areas shaded

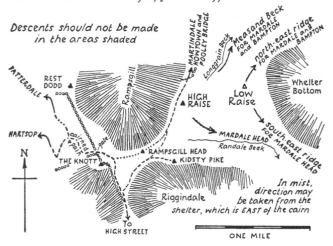

To PATTERDALE : An interesting and beautiful walk in good weather, but an anxious and complicated journey in bad. Note that Rampsgill Head must first be climbed before the descent properly commences, and that The Knott is rounded on its north side. *In bad weather, after crossing the wall between The Knott and Rest Dodd, descend directly to Hayeswater and Hartsop.*

To MARDALE : The north-east ridge particularly is a good way down, and the best if Bampton is the objective. The south-east ridge is rougher, with excellent views, but leads only to the uninhabited head of the valley: for the Haweswater Hotel, however, it is a useful route. *In mist, the streams are safe guides to the lakeside, but care is needed along Measand Beck.*

To MARTINDALE, HOWTOWN and POOLEY BRIDGE : Follow the ridge north, turning down left at Keasgill Head for Martindale and Howtown — and, in bad weather, for Pooley Bridge also. Consult the Wether Hill map.

THE VIEW

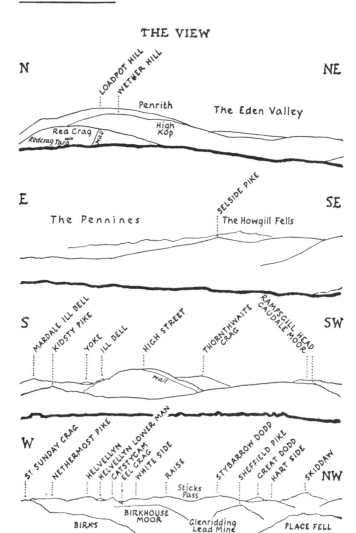

THE VIEW

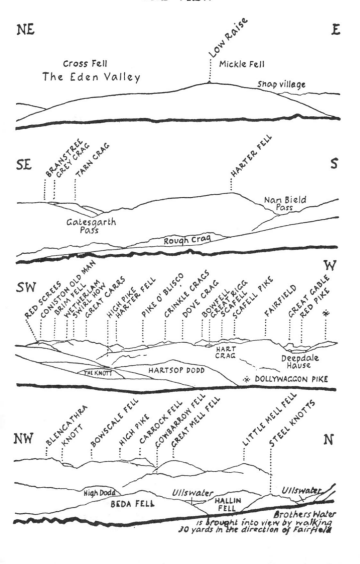

RIDGE ROUTES

To WETHER HILL, 2210' : 2¼ miles : NNE
Depression at 2150' : 100 feet of ascent
A long easy walk, safe in mist

Facing north, incline left to join the path (the old High Street), which continues, but not distinctly, to Wether Hill and beyond. It is usual to keep to the left of the wall as far as Redcrag Tarn and then cross it, but it is quicker, and in bad weather better, to follow it on the right. At the depression of Keasgill Head the path is badly cut away by a series of shallow ravines. Wether Hill has two tops ; the cairn is on the furthest.

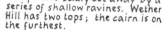

Redcrag Tarn
looking to High Raise and Rampsgill Head

To RAMPSGILL HEAD, 2581'
¾ mile : SW
Depression at 2450' :
140 feet of ascent
Easy, but needing care in mist

Join and follow the path to the grassy depression south-west. Here is a bifurcation : take the right fork and detour to look down the crags. In mist, keep left, on easy ground, if crags are encountered.

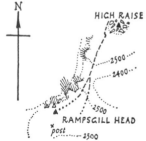

Whelter Beck and Whelter Crags

High Street

2718'

from the north ridge of Branstree

NATURAL FEATURES

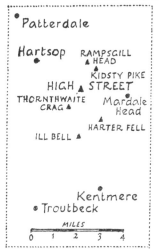

Patterdale

Hartsop   RAMPSGILL
            ▲ HEAD
              ▲ KIDSTY PIKE
HIGH ▲ STREET
THORNTHWAITE   Mardale
CRAG ▲   Head
          ▲ HARTER FELL
ILL BELL ▲

        Kentmere
  ● Troutbeck
        MILES
  0   1   2   3   4

Most of the high places in Lakeland have no mention in history books, and, until comparatively recent times, when enlightened men were inspired to climb upon them for pleasure and exercise, it was fashionable to regard them as objects of awe and terror, and their summits were rarely visited.   Not so High Street, which has been known and trodden, down through the ages, by a miscellany of travellers on an odd variety of missions: by marching soldiers, marauding brigands, carousing shepherds, officials of the Governments, and now by modern hikers. Its summit has been in turn a highway and a sports arena and a racecourse, as well as, as it is today, a grazing ground for sheep.

The long whale-backed crest of High Street attains a greater altitude than any other fell east of Kirkstone. Walking is easy on the grassy top: a factor that must have influenced the Roman surveyors to throw their road along it.   But High Street is much more than an elevated and featureless field, for its eastern flank, which falls precipitously from the flat top to enclose the splendid tarn of Blea Water in craggy arms, is a striking study in grandeur and wildness; on this side a straight narrow ridge running down to Mardale is particularly fine.   The western face drops roughly to Hayeswater. To north and south, high ground continues to subsidiary fells along the main ridge.

The River Kent has its birth in marshes on the south slope but most of the water draining from the fell flows northwards to Haweswater and Hayeswater.

Rough Crag
from
Long Stile

NATURAL FEATURES

The main High Street range
illustrating the complexity of the valley systems

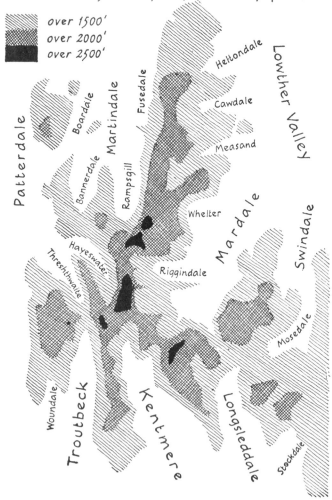

over 1500'
over 2000'
over 2500'

Patterdale

Boardale

Martindale

Bannerdale

Rampsgill

Fusedale

Heltondale

Cawdale

Measand

Lowther Valley

Whelter

Mardale

Swindale

Hayeswater

Threshthwaite

Riggindale

Mosedale

Woundale

Troutbeck

Kentmere

Longsleddale

Stockdale

MAP

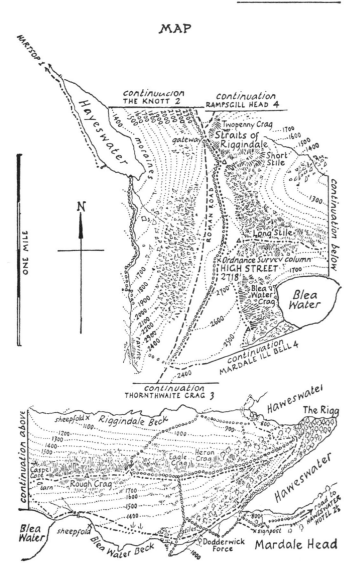

ASCENTS FROM PATTERDALE AND HARTSOP
2450 feet of ascent : 5½ miles from Patterdale
2300 feet of ascent : 3¾ miles from Hartsop

Proceed from the Straits of Riggindale to the summit not by the wall nor by the Roman Road (which are dull trudges) but by following the edge of the eastern face (which has excellent views) until the Ordnance Survey column comes into sight.

HIGH STREET

RAMPSGILL HEAD

Straits of Riggindale

2700

2600 — ROMAN ROAD — 2500

2500

2400

grass

2400

THE KNOTT

gateway

2300

2200

Rampsgill

REST DODD

2300

2200

2200

2100

scree gully

Enterprising pedestrians approaching from Hartsop may tackle High Street direct from the head of Hayeswater — but they will not enjoy the climb, which is steep, dull, and overburdened with scree.

2100

2000

2000

2000

1900

1900

peat hags

1800

1700

1600

1500 moraines

grass

Hayeswater

1900

Satura Crag

1400

Bannerdale

1800

1700

BROCK CRAGS

dam

For a diagram of the path from Hartsop to Hayeswater see The Knott 3

Buck Crag

gate

1800

1700

gate

1600

Angle Tarn

For a diagram of the ascent to Angle Tarn from Patterdale see Angletarn Pikes 5

HARTSOP 1

looking south-east

PATTERDALE 2

Two good viewpoints, only a few paces from the path but often missed, are (1) the main cairn on Satura Crag (view of Bannerdale), and (2) the tarn on the col below Rampsgill Head (view of Rampsgill)

This is the least exciting approach to High Street; it is, nevertheless, a very enjoyable walk, with a series of varied and beautiful views; and the tracking of the indistinct path, which has many unexpected turns and twists, is interesting throughout.

ASCENT FROM MARDALE

2050 feet of ascent   *3 miles from the road end*

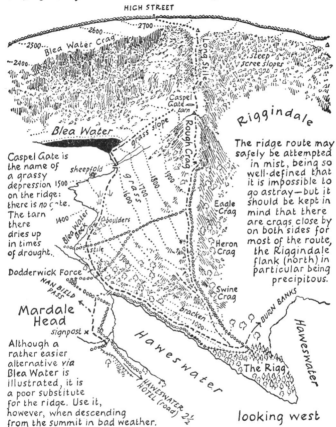

HIGH STREET

2600

2700

2500

Blea Water Crag

2400

Long Stile

steep scree slopes

Caspel Gate tarn

Riggindale

Blea Water

grass slope

Rough Crag

Caspel Gate is the name of a grassy depression 1500 on the ridge: there is no gate. The tarn there dries up in times of drought.

sheepfold

1800

1700

1600

grass

1400

Blea Water Beck

boulders

stile

Eagle Crag

Heron Crag

The ridge route may safely be attempted in mist, being so well-defined that it is impossible to go astray—but it should be kept in mind that there are crags close by on both sides for most of the route, the Riggindale flank (north) in particular being precipitous.

Dodderwick Force

NAN BIELD PASS

Swine Crag

bracken

1000

BURN BANKS

Mardale Head

signpost x

Haweswater

Haweswater

Although a rather easier alternative via Blea Water is illustrated, it is a poor substitute for the ridge. Use it, however, when descending from the summit in bad weather.

HAWESWATER HOTEL (road) 2½

The Rigg

looking west

The ridge of Rough Crag and the rocky stairway of Long Stile together form the connoisseur's route up High Street, the only route that discloses the finer characteristics of the fell. The ascent is a classic, leading directly along the crest of a long, straight ridge that permits of no variation from the valley to the summit. The views are excellent throughout.

ASCENT FROM TROUTBECK
2350 feet of ascent : 6 miles

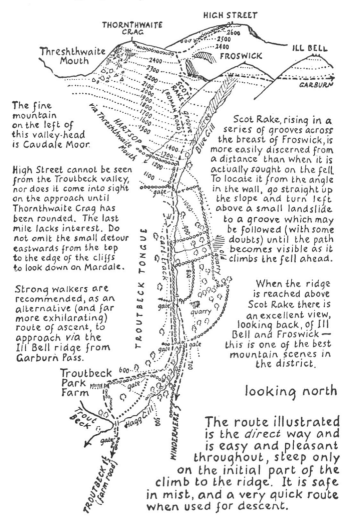

The fine mountain on the left of this valley-head is Caudale Moor.

High Street cannot be seen from the Troutbeck valley, nor does it come into sight on the approach until Thornthwaite Crag has been rounded. The last mile lacks interest. Do not omit the small detour eastwards from the top to the edge of the cliffs to look down on Mardale.

Strong walkers are recommended, as an alternative (and far more exhilarating) route of ascent, to approach via the Ill Bell ridge from Garburn Pass.

Scot Rake, rising in a series of grooves across the breast of Froswick, is more easily discerned from a distance than when it is actually sought on the fell. To locate it from the angle in the wall, go straight up the slope and turn left above a small landslide to a groove which may be followed (with some doubts) until the path becomes visible as it climbs the fell ahead.

When the ridge is reached above Scot Rake there is an excellent view, looking back, of Ill Bell and Froswick — this is one of the best mountain scenes in the district.

looking north

The route illustrated is the *direct* way and is easy and pleasant throughout, steep only on the initial part of the climb to the ridge. It is safe in mist, and a very quick route when used for descent.

ASCENT FROM KENTMERE
2300 feet of ascent
5½ miles via Hall Cove: 6 miles via Nan Bield Pass

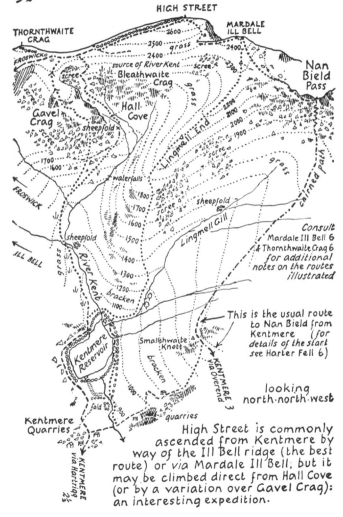

Consult
Mardale Ill Bell 6
& Thornthwaite Crag 6
for additional
notes on the routes
illustrated

This is the usual route
to Nan Bield from
Kentmere (for
details of the start
see Harter Fell 6)

looking
north-north-west

High Street is commonly
ascended from Kentmere by
way of the Ill Bell ridge (the best
route) or via Mardale Ill Bell; but it
may be climbed direct from Hall Cove
(or by a variation over Gavel Crag):
an interesting expedition.

Haweswater, from above Long Stile

Hayeswater, from the Roman Road

THE SUMMIT

The summit is barren of scenic interest, and only visitors of lively imagination will fully appreciate their surroundings. Any person so favoured may recline on the turf and witness, in his mind's eye, a varied pageant of history, for he has been preceded here, down the ages, by the ancient Britons who built their villages and forts in the valleys around; by the Roman cohorts marching between their garrisons at Ambleside and Brougham; by the Scots invaders who were repulsed on the Troutbeck slopes; by the shepherds, dalesmen and farmers who, centuries ago, made the summit their playground and feasting-place on the occasion of their annual meets; by racing horses (the summit is still named Racecourse Hill on the large-scale Ordnance Survey maps).....and let us not forget Dixon of immortal legend, whose great fall over the cliff while fox-hunting is an epic in enthusiasm.

Nowadays all is quiet here and only the rising larks disturb the stillness. A pleasant place, but — to those unfortunate folk with no imagination — so dull!

DESCENTS should be made only by the regular routes. It must be emphasised that there is only one direct way to Mardale — by Long Stile, the top of which is indicated by a cairn. Direct descents into Kentmere may lead to trouble, the best plan being to aim for Nan Bield Pass, in clear weather.

In mist, consult the maps. For Mardale, stick to the crest of Long Stile, but at Caspel Gate turn down right to Blea Water. Kentmere is best reached by descending into Hall Cove at a point 100 yards south east of the end of the High Street wall. Avoid the Hayeswater face.

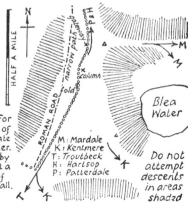

N

HALF A MILE

ROMAN ROAD

narrow path

fold

column

P & H

→ M

Blea Water

M: Mardale
K: Kentmere
T: Troutbeck
H: Hartsop
P: Patterdale

Do not attempt descents in areas shaded

THE VIEW

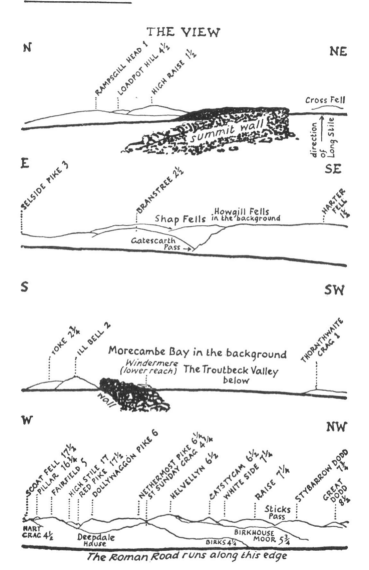

N — RAMPSGILL HEAD 1 — LOADPOT HILL 4½ — HIGH RAISE 1½ — NE

Cross Fell

summit wall

direction of Long Stile

E — SELSIDE PIKE 3 — BRANSTREE 2½ — SE

Shap Fells — Howgill Fells in the background — HARTER FELL 1¾

Gatescarth Pass →

S — TOKE 2¾ — ILL BELL 2 — SW

Morecambe Bay in the background
Windermere (lower reach)   The Troutbeck Valley below

wall

THORNTHWAITE CRAG 1

W — SCOAT FELL 17½ — PILLAR 16¾ — FAIRFIELD 5 — HIGH STILE 17 — RED PIKE 17½ — DOLLYWAGGON PIKE 6 — NETHERMOST PIKE 6½ — ST SUNDAY CRAG 4½ — HELVELLYN 6½ — CATSTYCAM 6½ — WHITE SIDE 7¼ — RAISE 7¾ — STYBARROW DODD 7½ — GREAT DODD 8½ — NW

HART CRAG 4½   Deepdale Hause   BIRKS 4¼   BIRKHOUSE MOOR 5¾   Sticks Pass

The Roman Road runs along this edge

THE VIEW

The figures following the names of fells
indicate distances in miles

NE   **E**

The Pennines in the background

View of Haweswater and Blea Water from this edge

SE   **S**

Ingleborough   KENTMERE PIKE 2½ ¾   MARDALE ILL BELL 3¾

Morecambe Bay
and the Kent Estuary

The Kentmere Valley
below

SW   **W**

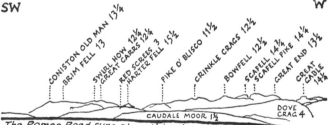

CONISTON OLD MAN 13¾ · BRIM FELL 13 · SWIRL HOW 12¾ · GREAT CARRS 12¼ · RED SCREES 3 · HARTER FELL 15½ · PIKE O' BLISCO 11½ · CRINKLE CRAGS 12½ · BOWFELL 12½ · SCAFELL 14¾ · SCAFELL PIKE 14¼ · GREAT END 13½ · GREAT GABLE 14¾ · DOVE CRAG 4

CAUDALE MOOR 1½

The Roman Road runs along this edge

NW   **N**

SKIDDAW 15¾ · HART SIDE 7¼ · ANGLETARN PIKES 3 · BLENCATHRA 12½ · PLACE FELL 4¼ · BOWSCALE FELL 13¾ · HIGH PIKE 16½ · CARROCK FELL 15¼ · REST DODD 1¾ · GREAT MELL FELL 9½ · THE KNOTT 1 · BEDA FELL 4 · LITTLE MELL FELL 8

View of Hayeswater from this edge

RIDGE ROUTES

To RAMPSGILL HEAD, 2581' : 1¼ miles : N then NE
Depression at 2340' : 250 feet of ascent
An easy and interesting walk

Follow the edge of the escarpment north to the narrow Straits of Riggindale. Beyond, watch for the divergence to the right from the main path, and bear left when the top of the fell is reached.

To MARDALE ILL BELL, 2496'
⁴⁄₅ mile : SE then ESE
Depression at 2350' : 150 feet of ascent
An easy walk with fine views

Follow the edge of the escarpment south-east — a cairn en route indicates an excellent view of Blea Water. Incline left when the marshy depression is crossed. In mist, there is likely to be some uncertainty beyond the depression.

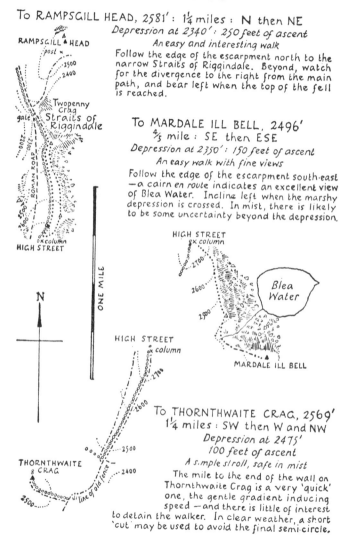

To THORNTHWAITE CRAG, 2569'
1¼ miles : SW then W and NW
Depression at 2475'
100 feet of ascent
A simple stroll, safe in mist

The mile to the end of the wall on Thornthwaite Crag is a very 'quick' one, the gentle gradient inducing speed — and there is little of interest to detain the walker. In clear weather, a short 'cut' may be used to avoid the final semi-circle.

High Street from Mardale Ill Bell

Blea Water Crag

Ill Bell

2476'

named 'Hill Bell' on the
2½" Ordnance Survey map

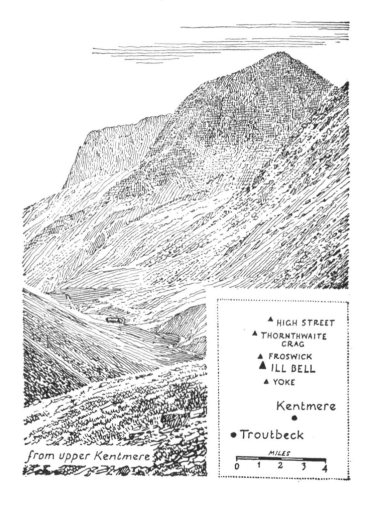

from upper Kentmere

▲ HIGH STREET
▲ THORNTHWAITE
   CRAG
▲ FROSWICK
▲ ILL BELL
▲ YOKE

Kentmere
●

● Troutbeck

MILES
0 1 2 3 4

NATURAL FEATURES

The graceful cone of Ill Bell is a familiar object to most residents of south Westmorland and those visitors who approach Lakeland by way of Kendal and Windermere, although few who know it by sight can give it a name and fewer still its correct name. It is the dominating height on a steep-sided ridge, running north to High Street from the foothills of Garburn, and forms a most effective and imposing barrier between the Troutbeck and upper Kentmere valleys. It is linked by easy slopes to its neighbours, Yoke and Froswick, but both flanks are excessively steep: the Kentmere side in particular is very rough and the aspect of the fell from the upper reaches of the valley is magnificent. Crags descend northwards from the small summit. Ill Bell is distinctive and of good appearance, its peaked shape making it easily identifiable. The ridge on which it stands is probably the most popular fell-walk east of Kirkstone.

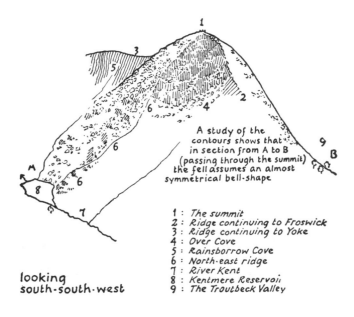

A study of the contours shows that in section from A to B (passing through the summit) the fell assumes an almost symmetrical bell-shape

1 : The summit
2 : Ridge continuing to Froswick
3 : Ridge continuing to Yoke
4 : Over Cove
5 : Rainsborrow Cove
6 : North-east ridge
7 : River Kent
8 : Kentmere Reservoir
9 : The Troutbeck Valley

looking
south-south-west

Ill Bell 3

MAP

The Ill Bell ridge, from Stile End

ASCENT FROM GARBURN PASS
1050 feet of ascent : 2½ miles

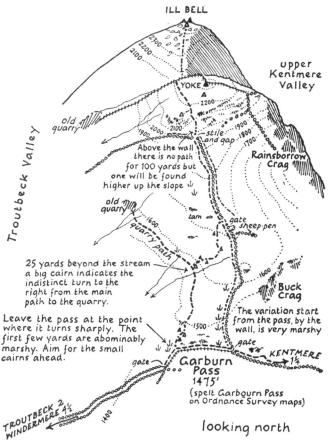

ILL BELL

upper Kentmere Valley

YOKE

old quarry

Troutbeck Valley

stile and gap

Rainsborrow Crag

Above the wall there is no path for 100 yards but one will be found higher up the slope ↓

old quarry

tarn

gate
sheep pen

quarry path

25 yards beyond the stream a big cairn indicates the indistinct turn to the right from the main path to the quarry.

Buck Crag

The variation start from the pass, by the wall, is very marshy.

Leave the pass at the point where it turns sharply. The first few yards are abominably marshy. Aim for the small cairns ahead.

gate

gate

Garburn Pass 1475'
(spelt Garbourn Pass on Ordnance Survey maps)

KENTMERE 1¼

TROUTBECK 2
WINDERMERE 4½

looking north

This is the obvious route to Ill Bell, and the only easy one. As far as Yoke it is a dull walk although the dreary foreground is relieved by the splendid views to the west. The route throughout is on grass, in places marshy to the 1800' contour.

ASCENT FROM
HAGG GILL, TROUTBECK
1700 feet of ascent

ASCENT FROM
KENTMERE RESERVOIR
1500 feet of ascent

ILL BELL

ILL BELL

2300

2200

FROSWICK

2100

YOKE

2000

grass

1900

1800

Quarry Brow

grass

1700

1600

1500

old quarry

ruins

1300

1200

intimidating gully

1100

ruins

spoil heap

ruin

gate

900

quarry path

ford

800

gate

Hagg Gill

TROUTBECK PARK FARM

This is the
second quarry in Hagg Gill (not
the first) and a most
interesting place it is. (The gates to it
have to be climbed). Slant up to the
left and ascend *beyond* the stream; a
long featureless slope follows. *In mist
the quarry is dangerous when descending*

looking north-east

2400

2300

2200

2100

2000

1900

1800

1700

Over Cove

1600

1500

1400

1300

scree

1200

north-east grass

1100

KENTMERE

1000

Kentmere
Reservoir

Proceed to the head of the reservoir
before turning up left to an obvious
ridge. The rough upper slopes appear
intimidating but steepness is the only
difficulty. In wintry conditions this
is a route for mountaineers only.

looking south-west

Ill Bell's continuously steep flanks are a challenge
to those who prefer to reach their objective by rough
scrambling, but walkers who walk for pleasure should
take the easy promenade from the top of Garburn.

THE SUMMIT

The walker who toils up to the top of Ill Bell may be pardoned for feeling that he has achieved a major climb that has played a part of some consequence in mountaineering history, for he finds himself confronted by an imposing array of fine cairns that would do credit to a Matterhorn. And in fact this is a real mountain-top, small in extent and very rough; it is one of the most distinctive summits in Lakeland. There are some traces of the wire fence that used to follow the ridge.

DESCENTS: The Troutbeck flank is steep, the Kentmere side is very steep and rough. Neither is suitable for descent, nor is there need to attempt them, for all destinations south are much more easily reached by way of the ridge to Garburn Pass.

In mist, Garburn Pass must be the objective. Join a path in the depression south of the summit and when it becomes indistinct keep on to a wall that continues to the Pass.

The main cairn

THE VIEW

Although higher fells northwards restrict the distant view in that direction, elsewhere it is good, the Scafells being prominent on the western skyline. Ill Bell is one of the classic 'stations' for viewing Windermere.

Principal Fells

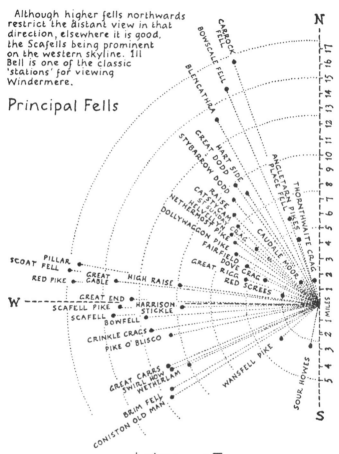

Lakes and Tarns

SSW: *Windermere*
SW: *Blelham Tarn*
NNW: A tiny strip of *Ullswater* is visible from the northern edge of the summit, 35 yards from main cairn.
E: *Kentmere Reservoir* is brought suddenly into view by walking 40 yards towards Harter Fell.

THE VIEW

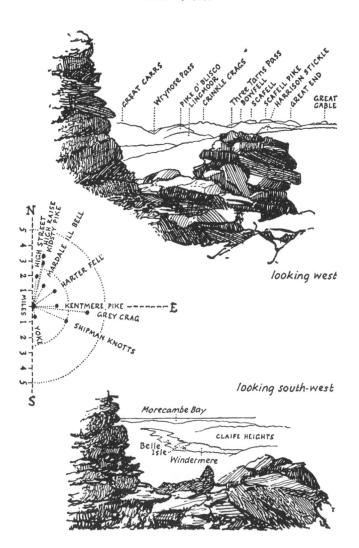

GREAT CARRS
Wrynose Pass
PIKE O' BLISCO
LINGMOOR
CRINKLE CRAGS
Three Tarns Pass
BOWFELL
SCAFELL
SCAFELL PIKE
HARRISON STICKLE
GREAT END
GREAT GABLE

looking west

N
5 4 3 2 1 MILES
HIGH STREET
HIGH RAISE
KIDSTY PIKE
MARDALE ILL BELL
HARTER FELL
KENTMERE PIKE -------- E
GREY CRAG
YOKE
SHIPMAN KNOTTS
1 2 3 4 5
S

looking south-west

Morecambe Bay
CLAIFE HEIGHTS
Belle Isle
Windermere

Thornthwaite Crag
and Froswick

Two views
from the
summit

Rainsborrow Cove
and Yoke

RIDGE ROUTES

To FROSWICK, 2359' : ⅔ mile : NW then N
Depression at 2075' : 285 feet of ascent
Rough at first, then easy walking

Turn west by the most northerly cairn, over stones (care needed in mist), and find a path going down north-west to the depression, beyond which is an easy climb on grass.

NOTE: The 1" Ordnance Survey map shows the height of the depression as *not less than 2100'*, the 2½" map as *not more than 2050'*. 2075' has been adopted here on the principle of moderation in all things.

ONE MILE

To YOKE, 2309' : ⅔ mile : S
Depression at 2180' : 130 feet of ascent
An easy walk, safe in mist

Descend by the southerly cairn. A faint track soon materialises and crosses the depression: at the far end, where it bifurcates, take the left branch along the edge of the escarpment. A wire fence is joined and leads over grass to the cairn. *In mist*, note that the cairn is adjacent to the *second* right-angle in the fence

Ill Bell and the head of Kentmere

HIGH
▲
STREET

● Mardale Head

HARTER FELL
▲

ILL BELL   KENTMERE
▲   ▲ PIKE   ▲ TARN
CRAG

▲
SHIPMAN KNOTTS

● Kentmere

Longsleddale ●

MILES
0   1   2   3   4

from Ill Bell
(north east ridge)

NATURAL FEATURES

A high ridge, a counterpart to the Ill Bell range across Kentmere, rises steeply to enclose the upper part of that valley on the east. This is the south ridge of Harter Fell, which, soon after leaving the parent summit, swells into the bare, rounded top of Kentmere Pike, a fell of some importance and of more significance to the inhabitants of the valley, as its name suggests, than Harter Fell itself. The Kentmere slope, wooded at its foot and craggy above, is of little interest, but the eastern flank is altogether of sterner stuff, falling precipitously into the narrow jaws of Longsleddale: a most impressive scene. Here, abrupt cliffs riven by deep gullies tower high above the crystal waters of the winding Sprint and give to the dalehead a savageness that contrasts strikingly with the placid sweetness of the Sadgill pastures just out of their shadow.

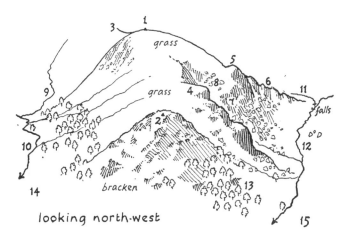

looking north-west

1: The summit
2: Shipman Knotts
3: Ridge continuing to Harter Fell
4: Goat Scar
5: Steel Pike
6: Steel Rigg
7: Raven Crag
8: Settle Earth
9: Ullstone Gill
10: River Kent
11: Wren Gill
12: River Sprint
13: Sadgill Woods
14: Kentmere
15: Longsleddale

Steel Pike, from the quarry road

looking down a scree gully, eastern flank

MAP

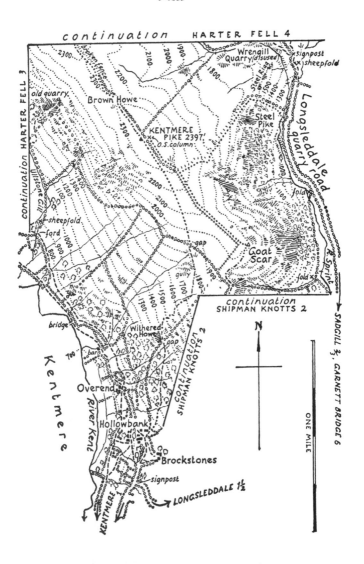

ASCENT FROM KENTMERE
1900 feet of ascent : 3 miles

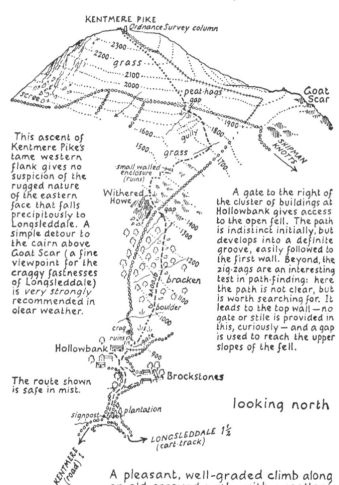

KENTMERE PIKE
Ordnance Survey column

2300
2200
grass
2100
2000
scree
peat hags
gap
Goat Scar
1900
SHIPMAN KNOTTS
1600
gully
1800
1500
grass
1700
small walled enclosure (ruins)
Withered Howe
gap
1400
1300
1200
bracken
1100
boulder
1000
crag
ruins
gate
Hollowbank
900
Brockstones
looking north
signpost
plantation
LONGSLEDDALE 1½ (cart-track)
KENTMERE (road) 1

This ascent of Kentmere Pike's tame western flank gives no suspicion of the rugged nature of the eastern face that falls precipitously to Longsleddale. A simple detour to the cairn above Goat Scar (a fine viewpoint for the craggy fastnesses of Longsleddale) is very strongly recommended in clear weather.

A gate to the right of the cluster of buildings at Hollowbank gives access to the open fell. The path is indistinct initially, but develops into a definite groove, easily followed to the first wall. Beyond, the zig-zags are an interesting test in path-finding: here the path is not clear, but is worth searching for. It leads to the top wall — no gate or stile is provided in this, curiously — and a gap is used to reach the upper slopes of the fell.

The route shown is safe in mist.

A pleasant, well-graded climb along an old grooved path, with excellent views of Kentmere, although the last mile is dull. This is the easiest way onto the Harter Fell ridge.

ASCENT FROM LONGSLEDDALE
1850 feet of ascent : 3 miles from Sadgill

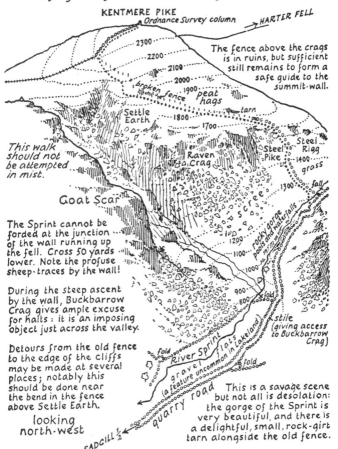

KENTMERE PIKE
Ordnance Survey column → HARTER FELL

2300
2200
2100
2000
broken fence 1900 peat hags
Settle Earth 1800 tarn
1700
Steel Pike Steel Rigg
Raven Crag 1400 grass
1700 fall
scree

The fence above the crags is in ruins, but sufficient still remains to form a safe guide to the summit wall.

Goat Scar

This walk should not be attempted in mist.

1200
1100
1000
900
800

rocky gorge pools and waterfalls

The Sprint cannot be forded at the junction of the wall running up the fell. Cross 50 yards lower. Note the profuse sheep-traces by the wall!

During the steep ascent by the wall, Buckbarrow Crag gives ample excuse for halts : it is an imposing object just across the valley.

Detours from the old fence to the edge of the cliffs may be made at several places; notably this should be done near the bend in the fence above Settle Earth.

looking north-west

fold
fold
River Sprint
gravel flats
(a feature uncommon in Lakeland)
fold
stile (giving access to Buckbarrow Crag)

This is a savage scene but not all is desolation: the gorge of the Sprint is very beautiful, and there is a delightful, small, rock-girt tarn alongside the old fence.

quarry road

SADGILL ½

This route has been devised for walkers who have a liking for impressive rock-scenery — it is the only practicable way up the rough eastern face, and it affords striking views of the crags, first from below then in profile and lastly from above.

THE SUMMIT

The top of the fell, an unattractive and uninteresting place, is robbed of any appeal it might otherwise have had by a high wall that bisects it from end to end.   A triangulation station of the Ordnance Survey in the form of a short column stands in the shelter of the east side of the wall, on a small rise, but its claim to occupy the highest point is disputed by a tiny pile of stones a few yards distant on the west side.

DESCENTS : To Kentmere : Anyone familiar with the grooved path going down to Hollowbank will have no difficulty in finding the start of it, at a break in the lower wall; strangers may not easily locate the gap and should instead continue by the ridge over Shipman Knotts to the Sadgill-Kentmere cart-track: *in mist, this route is safest.*   For Longsleddale, too, it is best to make this cart-track the objective. *Much of the Longsleddale flank is craggy and dangerous*, although the route described as an ascent on page 6 is a safe way off in clear weather.

The eastern face, with Harter Fell beyond, from Goat Scar

THE VIEW

The distant view of Lakeland is interrupted by the nearer heights across Kentmere; it is interesting to note that the summit-cone of Ill Bell exactly conceals Scafell Pike. More satisfactory prospects are south-east, towards the Pennines, and south-west, over Windermere to Morecambe Bay.

Principal Fells

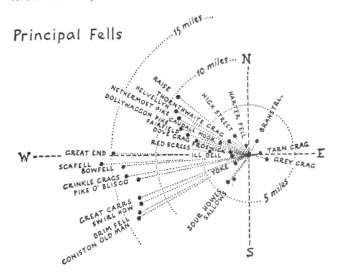

Lakes and Tarns
SSW : *Windermere*
Kentmere Reservoir is brought into view by walking 50 yards in the direction of Ill Bell.

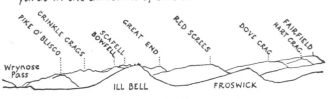

RIDGE ROUTES

To HARTER FELL, 2539': 1¼ miles
NNW then N

Depression at 2275': 275 feet of ascent

Easy walking on grass; safe in mist

Walls at first and then broken fences link the two summits (traces of the old fence on the broad top of Harter Fell are scarce) and indicate the route; intermittent path.

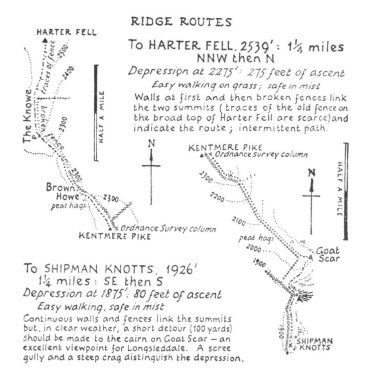

To SHIPMAN KNOTTS, 1926'
1¼ miles: SE then S

Depression at 1875': 80 feet of ascent

Easy walking, safe in mist

Continuous walls and fences link the summits but, in clear weather, a short detour (100 yards) should be made to the cairn on Goat Scar — an excellent viewpoint for Longsleddale. A scree gully and a steep crag distinguish the depression.

Branstree and the head of Longsleddale, from Goat Scar

Goat Scar
from
Longsleddale

Patterdale

Hartsop   ▲ HIGH RAISE
RAMPSGILL HEAD
▲ ▲ KIDSTY PIKE
Riggindale
▲ HIGH STREET

MILES
0   1   2   3   4

from Twopenny Crag

NATURAL FEATURES

Travellers on the road and railway at Shap, looking west to the long undulating skyline of the High Street range, will find their attention focussing on the most prominent feature there, the sharp peak of Kidsty Pike. This distinctive summit, which unmistakably identifies the fell whenever it is seen in profile, is formed by the sudden breaking of the gently-rising eastern slope in a precipice of crags and scree that falls very abruptly into the depths of Riggindale. The summit is the best feature of the fell. The Riggindale face is everywhere steep, but other slopes are easy except for an extensive area of rock halfway down the long eastern shoulder.

It is interesting to note that the raising of the level of Haweswater gave Kidsty Pike a 'footing' on the shore of the lake, for the first time — previously the confining becks of Randale and Riggindale united before reaching the lake, but now each enters as a separate feeder and the small strip of shore between is the new terminus of the fell.

The summit crags

MAP

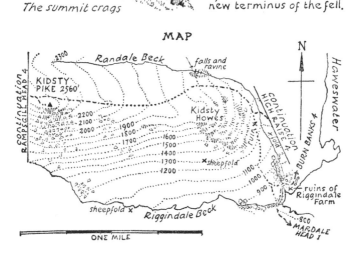

ASCENT FROM MARDALE
1900 feet of ascent : 3 miles from the road end

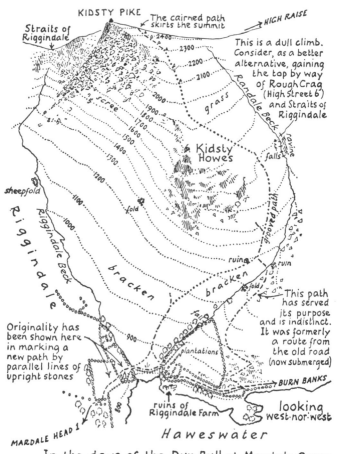

KIDSTY PIKE

The cairned path skirts the summit

→ HIGH RAISE

Straits of Riggindale

2400
2300
2200
2100
2000
1900
1800
1700
1600
1500
1400
1300
1200
1100
1000
900
800

This is a dull climb. Consider, as a better alternative, gaining the top by way of Rough Crag (High Street 6) and Straits of Riggindale

Randale Beck

grass

scree

Kidsty Howes

ravine

falls

sheepfold

Riggindale Beck

Riggindale

fold

bracken

bracken

ruin

ruin

fold

good path

This path has served its purpose and is indistinct. It was formerly a route from the old road (now submerged)

Originality has been shown here in marking a new path by parallel lines of upright stones

plantations

MARDALE HEAD

ruins of Riggindale Farm

Haweswater

BURN BANKS

looking west-nor'west

In the days of the Dun Bull at Mardale Green this was a favourite ascent. Now it is rarely used: the paths have gone to seed, and tough grass makes the climb laborious. The easiest route is that shown.

THE SUMMIT

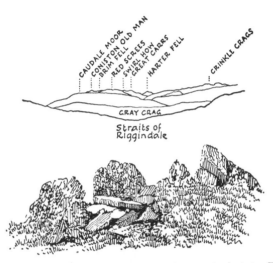

CAUDALE MOOR
CONISTON OLD MAN
BRIM FELL
RED SCREES
SWIRL HOW
GREAT CARRS
HARTER FELL
CRINKLE CRAGS

GRAY CRAG

Straits of
Riggindale

The summit is an eyrie perched high above Riggindale. The small cairn stands on grass amongst the boulders of the top pedestal, and crags are immediately below. The situation is dramatic. A narrow track leads to it from the north west.

DESCENTS: For Patterdale or Hartsop, make a bee-line over Rampsgill Head, crossing it near the old signpost, and join the path below the Knott. For Mardale (if accommodation has been reserved) walk north to join a cairned track skirting the summit. Obviously there is no direct way into Riggindale.

In mist, keep to the Straits of Riggindale track if bound for Patterdale or Hartsop, the path for which is joined near a wall. For Mardale, when the cairned track peters out bear half-left and descend with the music of Randale Beck kept a furlong away on the left hand to avoid ravines.

RIDGE ROUTE

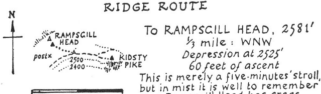

N

RAMPSGILL
HEAD

post x

2500
2400

KIDSTY
PIKE

HALF A MILE

To RAMPSGILL HEAD, 2581'
⅓ mile : WNW
Depression at 2525'
60 feet of ascent
This is merely a five-minutes'stroll, but in mist it is well to remember that Rampsgill Head has crags.

THE VIEW

The bulky masses of High Street, Rampsgill Head and High Raise, all in close proximity, cut out big slices of the distant panorama; but in those directions where the view is unrestricted, it is good.

Principal Fells

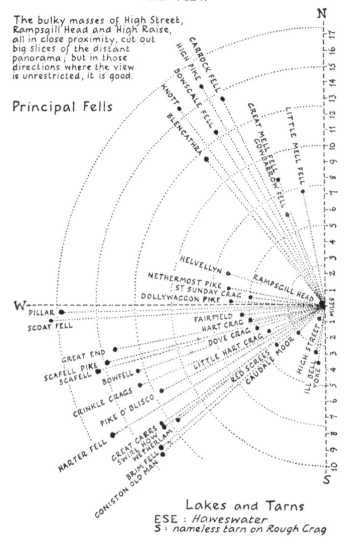

N

CARROCK FELL
HIGH PIKE
BOWSCALE FELL
KNOTT
BLENCATHRA
GREAT MELL FELL
COWBARROW FELL
LITTLE MELL FELL

HELVELLYN
NETHERMOST PIKE
ST SUNDAY CRAG
DOLLYWAGGON PIKE
RAMPSGILL HEAD

W

PILLAR
SCOAT FELL
FAIRFIELD
HART CRAG
DOVE CRAG
LITTLE HART CRAG
RED SCREES
CAUDALE MOOR
HIGH STREET
ILL BELL
YOKE

GREAT END
SCAFELL PIKE
SCAFELL
BOWFELL
CRINKLE CRAGS
PIKE O'BLISCO
GREAT CARRS
SWIRL HOW
WETHERLAM
BRIM FELL
CONISTON OLD MAN
HARTER FELL

S

Lakes and Tarns

ESE: *Haweswater*
S: *nameless tarn on Rough Crag*

THE VIEW

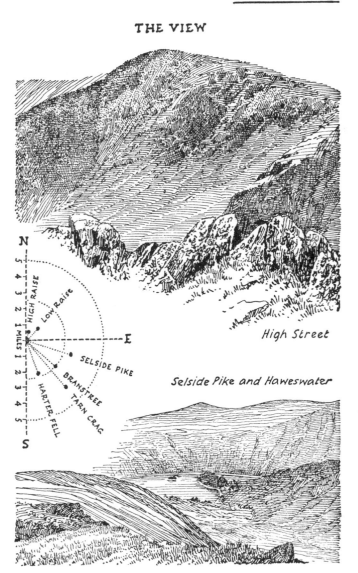

High Street

Selside Pike and Haweswater

The Knott

2423'

- Patterdale

Hartsop
- ▲ HIGH RAISE
  ▲ ▲ RAMPSGILL HEAD
THE KNOTT
  ▲ HIGH STREET

MILES
0 1 2 3 4

from Hayeswater Gill

NATURAL FEATURES

The steep western slope descending from Rampsgill Head is arrested below the summit, just as the fall is gathering impetus, by a protuberance that takes the shape of a small conical hill. This is the Knott, a key point for walkers in this area, and although its short side rises barely a hundred feet from the main fell, its appearance is imposing when seen from other directions and especially when approached from the Hartsop valley. Fans of scree litter its western flank, which goes down steeply to Hayeswater; a tremendous scree gully here is the Knott's one interesting feature.

MAP

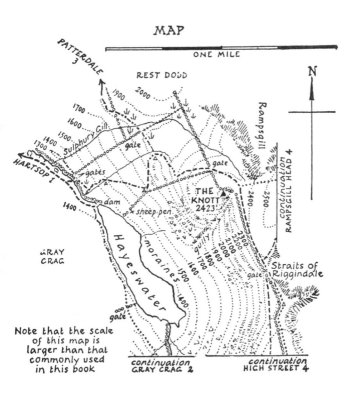

ONE MILE

N

PATTERDALE 3

REST DODD

Rampsgill

1900
2000

1700
1600
1500
1400
1300

sulphury Gill

gate

CONTINUATION
RAMPSGILL HEAD 4

HARTSOP 1

gates

gate

2400
2500

1400

dam

sheep pen

THE KNOTT
2423'

GRAY CRAG

Hayeswater

moraines

gully

2300
2200
2100
2000
1900
1800
1700
1600
1500
1400

Straits of
Riggindale

gate

gate

Note that the scale of this map is larger than that commonly used in this book

continuation
GRAY CRAG 2

continuation
HIGH STREET 4

ASCENT FROM HARTSOP
1850 feet of ascent : 2 miles

THE KNOTT

HIGH STREET

REST DODD

gate

2300
2200
2100   scree
2000
1900
1800
1700

scree

scree gully

peat-hags

gate

PATTERDALE 3

1700

1600

Sulphury Gill

1500

1400

1300

Prison Gill

GRAY CRAG

sheep-pen

dam ← Hayeswater

Sulphury Gill descends in a series of cascades

gates

ford

cascades

1300
1200

The rickety footbridge over the stile near the filter house is (at the time of writing) unexpectedly safe
STOP PRESS! —
New bridge. 1956

BROCK CRAGS

gate
stile
filter house

gate   1100
1000

1200

1100

gate

Wath Bridge

barn

Pasture Beck

THRESHTHWAITE MOUTH

Normally the path on the right side of the gill from Wath Bridge is best, but if the beck is in spate the ford may be impassable and it is then advisable to keep on the left side of the gill past the filter house

1000

900

800

Hayeswater Gill

ruin

gate
ruin

Incidentally, this route is the quickest way to the High Street from the Kirkstone road

gate   Walker Bridge

Low Hartsop

looking east

As far as Hayeswater, this is a fine approach; beyond, it deteriorates into a dull trudge.

THE SUMMIT

HIGH RAISE   RAMPSGILL HEAD

The small top of the fell is without interest except for some bouldery excavations overlooking the gully on the south which seem artificial. A wall crosses the summit, forming an angle; a few paces away is the cairn. **DESCENTS** : Follow the wall either way to join the path.

THE VIEW

Eastwards the view is severely confined to the High Street range, but in other directions it is excellent

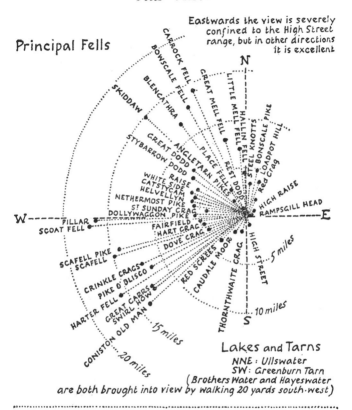

Principal Fells

CARROCK FELL
BOWSCALE FELL
BLENCATHRA
SKIDDAW
GREAT MELL FELL
LITTLE MELL FELL
N
HALLIN FELL
STEEL KNOTTS
BONSCALE PIKE
LOADPOT HILL
Red Crag
ANGLETARN PIKES
GREAT DODD
PLACE FELL
STYBARROW DODD
REST DODD
RAISE
WHITE SIDE
CATSTYCAM
HELVELLYN
NETHERMOST PIKE
St SUNDAY CRAG
DOLLYWAGGON PIKE
HIGH RAISE
PILLAR
SCOAT FELL
W
RAMPSGILL HEAD
E
FAIRFIELD
HART CRAG
DOVE CRAG
SCAFELL PIKE
SCAFELL
RED SCREES
HIGH STREET
5 miles
CRINKLE CRAGS
PIKE O'BLISCO
CAUDALE MOOR
HARTER FELL
GREAT CARRS
SWIRL HOW
10 miles
THORNTHWAITE CRAG
CONISTON OLD MAN
15 miles
S
20 miles

Lakes and Tarns

NNE : Ullswater
SW : Greenburn Tarn
(Brothers Water and Hayeswater are both brought into view by walking 20 yards south-west)

RIDGE ROUTES

To RAMPSGILL HEAD, 2581': ⅓ mile : E
Depression at 2360': 225 feet of ascent
An easy climb. Avoid cliffs (on left) in mist

To REST DODD, 2278': ¾ mile : NNW
Depression at 1925': 360 feet of ascent
A straightforward walk, following the wall until it turns left, then directly ahead to the top

RAMPSGILL HEAD
2500
2400
2100
2000
THE KNOTT
2300
REST DODD
gate
N
QUARTER MILE

Loadpot Hill

from Sandwick

• Pooley Bridge
  •
  Askham

Helton •

▲ ARTHUR'S PIKE

• Howtown

LOADPOT
▲ HILL
              Bampton •

▲ WETHER HILL

MILES
0   1   2   3   4

The beacon on The Pen

NATURAL FEATURES

The High Street range, narrow-waisted at the impressive Straits of Rigginedale, thereafter develops buxom girth as it proceeds north. Although the western flank continues steep to its extremity on Arthur's Pike, the eastern slopes descend gradually and irresolutely, halting often in wide plateaux and covering a considerable tract of moorland that is intersected by a succession of deep-cut gills, all of which join the main lateral valley of Mardale and the River Lowther. Nowhere is this characteristic manifest more than in Loadpot Hill, and because Loadpot Hill is the last of the principal eminences of the range it also has northern slopes, no less extensive, which exhibit the same reluctance to depart from the high places: hence the gradients are easy, with subsidiary hillocks arresting the decline. By Lakeland standards (which demand at least a glimpse of *rock* in every scene) territory of this type is uninteresting, for all hereabouts is tough grass and heather except for the single shattered scree-rash of Brock Crag, above Fusedale; yet there is a haunting attractiveness about these far-flung rolling expanses. There is the appearance of desolation, but no place is desolate that harbours so much life: in addition to the inevitable sheep, hardy fell ponies roam and graze at will, summer and winter alike, and the Martindale deer often cross the watershed; in springtime especially, the number and variety of birds is quite unusual for the fells. There is little to disturb these creatures. Man is not the enemy, only the fox and the buzzard. Loadpot Hill is a natural sanctuary for all wild life.

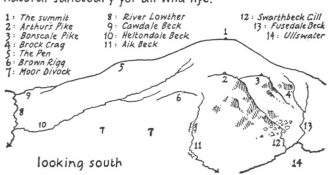

1 : The summit
2 : Arthur's Pike
3 : Bonscale Pike
4 : Brock Crag
5 : The Pen
6 : Brown Rigg
7 : Moor Divock

8 : River Lowther
9 : Cawdale Beck
10 : Heltondale Beck
11 : Aik Beck

12 : Swarthbeck Gill
13 : Fusedale Beck
14 : Ullswater

looking south

Cop Stone
and an oddly-sited
signpost

The antiquities
and oddities of
Moor Divock

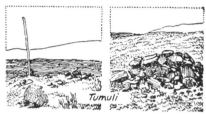

Tumuli

Man may (and does) neglect Loadpot Hill nowadays, but it was not always so. There are evidences in plenty of the esteem with which it has been regarded in the past. Even before the Romans traversed it with their High Street, its slopes were the home and meeting-place of man. There is a stone circle created by human agency near the headwaters of Swarthbeck Gill, Druidical remains and other curiosities in surprising profusion on Moor Divock on the 1050' contour, while, nearer our own time, men have laboured

A boundary stone

to erect an elaborate system of parochial boundary stones and posts along Loadpot's top and down its flanks. (It is a contrasting commentary on a modern enlightened age that the most recent erections on the Moor are shooting-hides from which the harmless and helpless grouse may be killed and crippled) And no other Lakeland fell has a domestic chimney-stack and a concrete living-room floor almost on its summit!

A boundary post

Moor Divock is of very special interest to the antiquarian and archæologist, and has long been a happy hunting-ground for them. The geologist will be concerned with investigating the crater-like hollows or sinkholes (locally known as swallows), which incidentally often contain carcasses and skeletons. The humbler pedestrian, not versed in the sciences, will be impressed by the spaciousness and loneliness of the scene and the excellence of its principal path.

Stone Circles

MAP

Loadpot Hill is the principal eminence of the High Street range at the northern extremity, and is extensive in area. Five pages of maps are necessary in order to show fully the main approaches to the fell from the villages at its base.

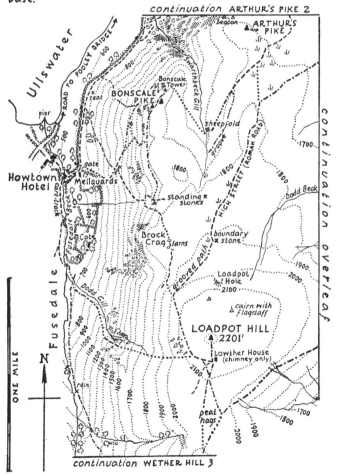

MAP

Reference should be made to the note at the top of page 8 before this map is consulted.

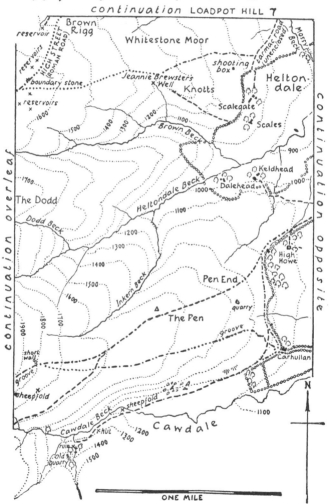

continuation LOADPOT HILL 7

ONE MILE

MAP

Reference should be made to the note at the top of page 8 before this map is consulted.

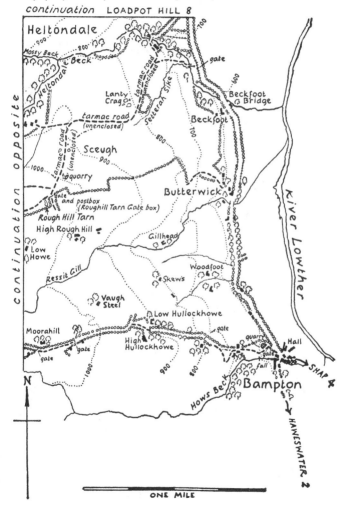

continuation LOADPOT HILL 8

Heltondale

Mossy Beck

Heltondale Beck

Lanty Crag

Sceugh

quarry

tarmac road (unenclosed)

tarmac road (unenclosed)

gate and postbox (Roughill Tarn Gate box)

Rough Hill Tarn

High Rough Hill

Low Howe

Ressit Gill

Vaugh Steel

Moorahill

gate

gate

High Hullockhowe

Low Hullockhowe

Skews

Gillhead

Butterwick

Woodfoot

Beckfoot

Beckfoot Bridge

gate

River Lowther

quarry

Hall

gate

fall

Bampton

Hows Beck

SHAP 4

HAWESWATER 2

800

700

700

600

600

900

1000

700

1000

900

800

Setterah Sike

continuation opposite

N

ONE MILE

MAP

Reference should be made to the note at the top
of page 8 before this map is consulted.

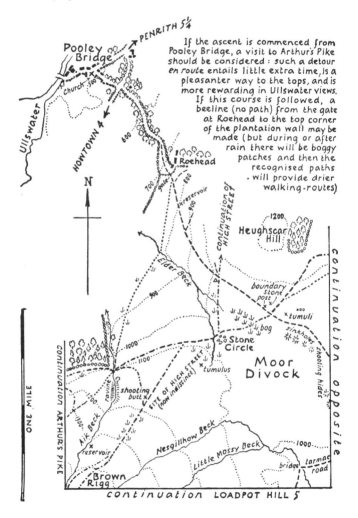

If the ascent is commenced from
Pooley Bridge, a visit to Arthur's Pike
should be considered: such a detour
en route entails little extra time, is a
pleasanter way to the tops, and is
more rewarding in Ullswater views.
If this course is followed, a
beeline (no path) from the gate
at Roehead to the top corner
of the plantation wall may be
made (but during or after
rain there will be boggy
patches and then the
recognised paths
will provide drier
walking-routes)

MAP

NOTE on the Loadpot Hill maps:

Walkers bound for the summit, especially from the north and east, may have difficulty in finding access to the fell : routes cannot be determined by observation from valley-level because of intervening tracts of cultivated farmland, which must be traversed before open ground is reached. A maze of byways and walled enclosures and farmsteads complicates the approaches. Many variations may be made, but the accompanying maps illustrate only the most direct routes, and, to depict them more clearly, *much unnecessary detail in the cultivated areas has been omitted.*

Those walkers who, like the author, do not enjoy encounters with cows and young bulls and the sundry other mammals that commonly frequent confined farmyards will be relieved to learn that the routes illustrated have been specially selected to reduce this possibility to a minimum, and only at one place (Carhullan) is it necessary to pass through a farmyard.

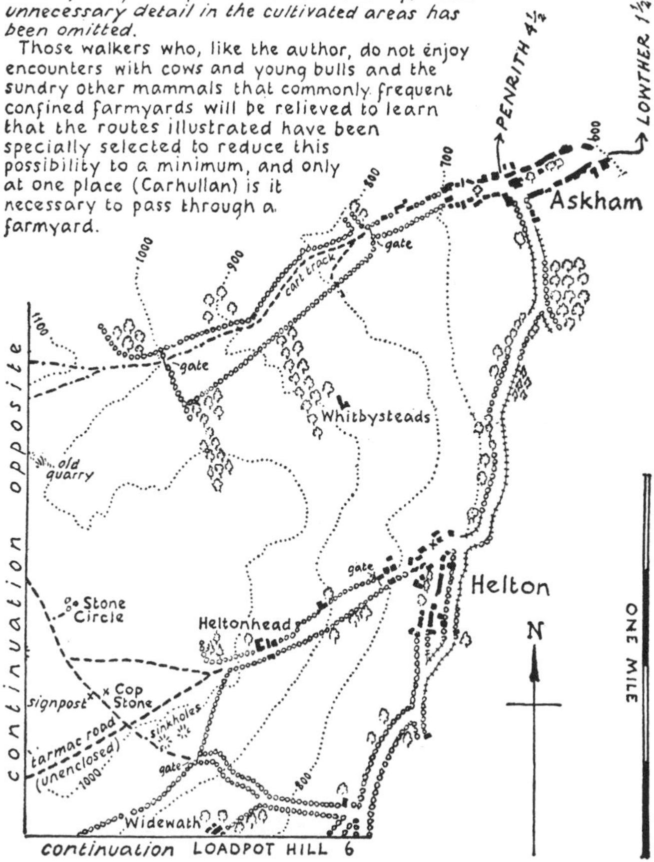

PENRITH 4¼

LOWTHER 1½

600

700

800

900

1000

1000

1100

Askham

carl track

gate

gate

Whitbysteads

old quarry

continuation opposite

Stone Circle

Heltonhead

gate

Helton

N

ONE MILE

signpost

Cop Stone

tarmac road (unenclosed)

1000

sinkholes

gate

Widewath

continuation LOADPOT HILL 6

ASCENTS FROM BAMPTON AND HELTON
1650 feet of ascent
4½ miles from Bampton; 5½ miles from Helton

LOADPOT HILL

NETHER HILL — chimney — grass — 2100

MOOR DIVOCK

2000

wall 1900

1800

× sheep fold

grass

1800
1700
1600
1500
1400
1300
1200
1100

Black fell ponies graze on the upper slopes. They are docile

The Pen

△ beacon

Inkern Beck

Heltondale Beck

heather

heather

quarry

Pen End

Cawdale Beck

Cawdale

There is one breach in the cultivated land where the moor comes down almost to the road: the Helton route traverses this

Carhullan

1100

Moorahill

High Howe

gate

Rough Hill Tarn

unenclosed tarmac road

rough pasture

gate

1000

Roughill Tarn Gate · postbox

Roughill Tarn Gate postbox

Sceugh

road

rough pasture

Lanty Crag

tarmac road

Low Hullockhowe

gate

900

800

Hows Beck

gate

700

cultivated farmland

MOOR DIVOCK

tarn

700

footbridge

Beckfoot

gate

HELTON

waterfall

quarry

gate

Beckfoot Bridge

½

Bampton

The first field on the approach from Bampton —a common— has many charming waterfalls, and more rock than will be met on the whole of the rest of the walk

looking west

The Helton route is rather the more interesting of the two illustrated, but both are pleasant walks in quiet, unexciting surroundings. The upper slopes are simple and very easy, but deceptively long.

ASCENT FROM MOOR DIVOCK
1300 feet of ascent : 4½ miles

Full route from POOLEY BRIDGE
1800 feet of ascent : 6 miles

Full route from ASKHAM
1600 feet of ascent : 6½ miles

LOADPOT HILL

(chimney on south side)

grass · 2100

2000 · Loadpot Hole

grass

groove

boundary stone × · 1900

Fell ponies are likely to be seen on these slopes where they live all the year. When the fell is under deep snow they are fed from the farms. Many go to work in the coal-pits.

Standing Stones (only one remains standing — and that one leans badly)

rutted path

HIGH STREET (ROMAN ROAD) · 1800

Swarthbeck Gill

The gradients are everywhere simple. Even the most decrepit hiker will surmount them with ease.

Bridge in Heltondale

1700

reservoirs

sheepfold

ARTHUR'S PIKE · beacon

All the reservoirs shown on this diagram are covered. But not Jeannie's delectable chalice!

Heltondale

Jeannie Brewster's Well

grass

× boundary stone

× reservoirs

1600

× reservoir

grass path in heather

White Knott

shooting box

1000 · gorse · 1300 · 1200 · 1100

1400 · 1500

Brown Rigg

heather

× reservoir

grass path in heather

bracken

HOWTOWN

HELTON · tarmac road (unenclosed) · bridge

signpost

Cop Stone ×

heather

Aik Beck

game track

shooting butt

ravine

1100

This is positively the worst bog on any regular Lakeland path. Avoid it!

Stone Circle

Hole Holes

sinkholes

Pulpit Holes

bog

Stone Circle

The place to turn off the Howtown path is NOT distinct. Do this 300 yards beyond the Circle

Moor Divock

wide path

tumuli

bracken

stone post (boundary)

ASKHAM

bracken

△ cairn

Elder Beck

good wide path · POOLEY BRIDGE

looking south-south-west

This is not a walk for a wet or misty day, and ample time should be allowed. The High Street of the Romans is now, at best, only a line of ruts in the grass. The ascent *via* Arthur's Pike is recommended for its superior views.

ASCENT FROM HOWTOWN
1750 feet of ascent : 2¼ miles

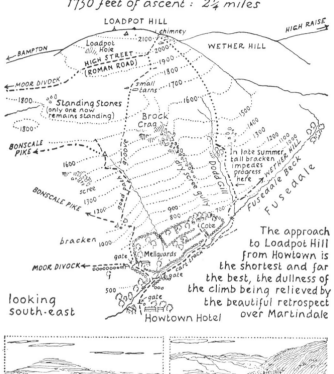

LOADPOT HILL

HIGH RAISE

chimney

2100

Loadpot
Hole

2000

WETHER HILL

BAMPTON

HIGH STREET
(ROMAN ROAD)

1900

1800

MOOR DIVOCK

small
tarns

1700

1800

Standing Stones
(only one now
remains standing)

1600

1500

Brock
Crag

1400

1300

1200 1100 1000

1800

BONSCALE
PIKE

In late summer,
tall bracken
impedes
progress
here

WETHER HILL

Fusedale Beck

FUSEDALE

1600

groove

scree

dry scree gully

Dodd Gill

BONSCALE PIKE

1300

700

1200

900

800

Cote

bracken 1000

gate Mellguards

cart track

MOOR DIVOCK

gate

500

gate

looking
south-east

Howtown Hotel

The approach
to Loadpot Hill
from Howtown is
the shortest and far
the best, the dullness of
the climb being relieved by
the beautiful retrospect
over Martindale

Fusedale and
Ullswater
from Dodd Gill

Brock Crag
and Ullswater

THE SUMMIT

Reference has already been made to the attention paid to Loadpot Hill since ancient times, and this is also manifest in the cairn on the summit — somebody, sometime, has gone to the trouble to collect, somewhere, a number of handsome stones foreign to the immediate neighbourhood, all prominently displaying a glittering quartz content, and transport them, somehow, to the highest point; these form a cairn around the base of a boundary-stone; which itself bears the inscriptions of a benchmark (⩚) and a capital letter L (probably for Lowther).

Apart from this cairn, and another adorned with a flagstaff, the summit is unremarkable. All is grass and all is flat, and more like a 30-acre field than a mountain top.

DESCENTS: Descents may be made easily and safely in any direction. (Loadpot *Hole* is not a hazard to avoid — it is not a hole one can fall into but a shallow landslip, which, because it faces north, holds the last snow on the fell every spring).

In mist, the walker should not be here at all, but if he is his best plan is probably to descend westwards to the High Street (only a rut in the grass) and follow it to Moor Divock: not an easy task. *If conditions are bad* cross High Street and, still heading west, go down the steepening bracken slopes into Fusedale (for Howtown)

Just below and south of the summit is the one landmark that distinguishes this fell from all others. This is the chimney of Lowther House, a former shooting-lodge, with stables: the wooden structure has now been dismantled and taken away, but the stone stack of the chimney, now an ornament of no use, still points forlornly to the sky.

Chimney, Lowther House

THE VIEW

Principal Fells

One half of the panorama is Lakeland, dominated by the high, imposing range of Helvellyn; the other half is Pennine, with Cross Fell and its satellites prominent

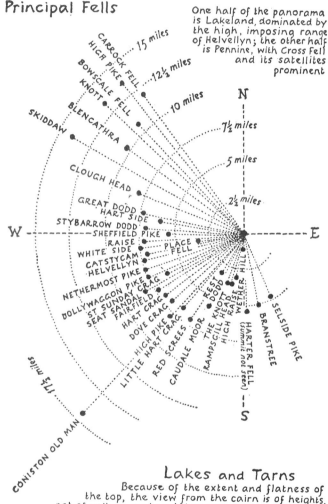

CARROCK FELL
HIGH PIKE
BOWSCALE FELL
KNOTT
BLENCATHRA
SKIDDAW
CLOUGH HEAD
GREAT DODD
HART SIDE
STYBARROW DODD
SHEFFIELD PIKE
RAISE
WHITE SIDE
CATSTYCAM
HELVELLYN
NETHERMOST PIKE
DOLLYWAGGON PIKE
ST SUNDAY CRAG
SEAT SANDAL
FAIRFIELD
HART CRAG
DOVE CRAG
HIGH PIKE
LITTLE HART CRAG
RED SCREES
CAUDALE MOOR
RAMPSGILL HEAD
THE KNOTT
HIGH RAISE
KIDSTY
DODD
REST
WETHER HILL
PLACE FELL
HARTER FELL (summit not seen)
BRANSTREE
SELSIDE PIKE
CONISTON OLD MAN

15 miles
12½ miles
10 miles
7½ miles
5 miles
2½ miles
17½ miles

N
E
S
W

Lakes and Tarns

Because of the extent and flatness of the top, the view from the cairn is of heights, not of valleys, and no lakes are visible. Ullswater, however, can be seen by walking 150 yards towards the west

RIDGE ROUTES

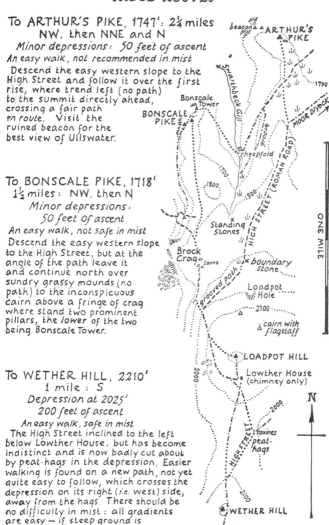

To ARTHUR'S PIKE, 1747': 2¼ miles NW, then NNE and N
Minor depressions: 50 feet of ascent
An easy walk, not recommended in mist

Descend the easy western slope to the High Street and follow it over the first rise, where trend left (no path) to the summit directly ahead, crossing a fair path en route. Visit the ruined beacon for the best view of Ullswater.

To BONSCALE PIKE, 1718'
1½ miles: NW, then N
Minor depressions: 50 feet of ascent
An easy walk, not safe in mist

Descend the easy western slope to the High Street, but at the angle of the path leave it and continue north over sundry grassy mounds (no path) to the inconspicuous cairn above a fringe of crag where stand two prominent pillars, the *lower* of the two being Bonscale Tower.

To WETHER HILL, 2210'
1 mile: S
Depression at 2025'
200 feet of ascent

An easy walk, safe in mist

The High Street inclined to the left below Lowther House, but has become indistinct and is now badly cut about by peat-hags in the depression. Easier walking is found on a new path, not yet quite easy to follow, which crosses the depression on its right (i.e. west) side, away from the hags. There should be no difficulty in mist: all gradients are easy — if steep ground is encountered the route is lost.

Mardale Ill Bell

2496'

from the north ridge of
Branstree

HIGH STREET
▲

● Mardale
Head

MARDALE
ILL BELL ▲

▲ HARTER FELL

▲ ILL BELL

● Kentmere

MILES

0   1   2   3   4

NATURAL FEATURES

Mardale Ill Bell has received scant mention in Lakeland literature, and admittedly is mainly of nondescript appearance, yet one aspect of the fell is particularly good and appeals on sight to all who aspire to a little mild mountaineering. This is to the north-east, where a boulder-strewn shoulder leaves the summit and soon divides into two craggy ridges, enclosing a rocky corrie; the rugged surroundings on this side are greatly enhanced in impressiveness by the two splendid tarns of Blea Water (below High Street) and Small Water (below Harter Fell), each of them occupying a volcanic crater and deeply inurned amongst crags. These tarns, with their streams, are collectively known as Mardale Waters, and greatly contribute to the fine scenic quality of this typical Lakeland landscape.

To the west the fell merges gently and dully into High Street, with a fringe of crag throughout on the north; and south of the linking high ground is a wall of steep rock, Bleathwaite Crag, bounding the silent hollow of Hall Cove, the birthplace of the River Kent. On the south also is the most pronounced shoulder of the fell, Lingmell End, thrusting far into the valley of Kentmere, and from it descends a short spur to the top of Nan Bield Pass.

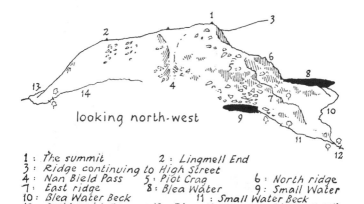

looking north-west

1 : The summit   2 : Lingmell End
3 : Ridge continuing to High Street
4 : Nan Bield Pass   5 : Piot Crag   6 : North ridge
7 : East ridge   8 : Blea Water   9 : Small Water
10: Blea Water Beck   11 : Small Water Beck
12: Dodderwick Force   13 : River Kent   14 : Lingmell Gill

Waterfalls, River Kent below Hall Cove

Dodderwick Force

The north face from Blea Water

MAP

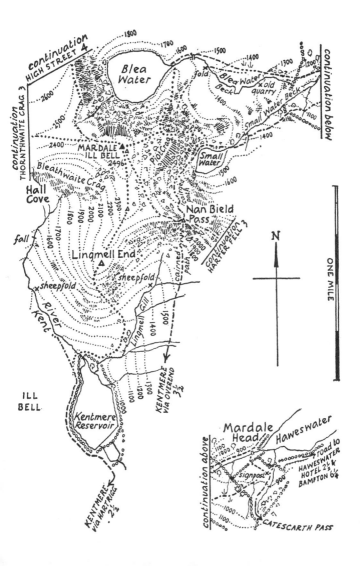

ASCENT FROM MARDALE
1700 feet of ascent : 2 miles from the road end

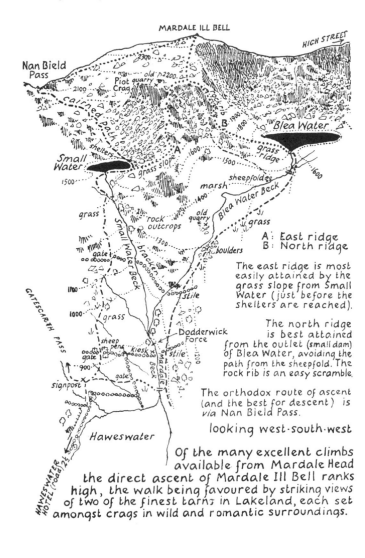

MARDALE ILL BELL

HIGH STREET

Nan Bield Pass

cairned path

Piot quarry Crag

2100

2200

2300

Blea Water

2000

1900

1800

A

B

grass ridge

Small Water

1500

shelters

grass slope

1600

1500

1600

sheepfolds

marsh

Blea Water Beck

grass

grass

1400

old quarry

rock outcrops

1300

boulders

Small Water Beck

bracken

gate

gate

1100

1000

grass

Dodderwick Force

stile

stile

sheep pens

kiosk

gate

900

gate

signpost

Mardale Beck

Haweswater

GATESCARTH PASS

HAWESWATER HOTEL (ROAD) 2¼

A: East ridge
B: North ridge

The east ridge is most easily attained by the grass slope from Small Water (just before the shelters are reached).

The north ridge is best attained from the outlet (small dam) of Blea Water, avoiding the path from the sheepfold. The rock rib is an easy scramble.

The orthodox route of ascent (and the best for descent) is via Nan Bield Pass.

looking west·south·west

Of the many excellent climbs available from Mardale Head the direct ascent of Mardale Ill Bell ranks high, the walk being favoured by striking views of two of the finest tarns in Lakeland, each set amongst crags in wild and romantic surroundings.

ASCENT FROM KENTMERE
2100 feet of ascent : 4¾ miles

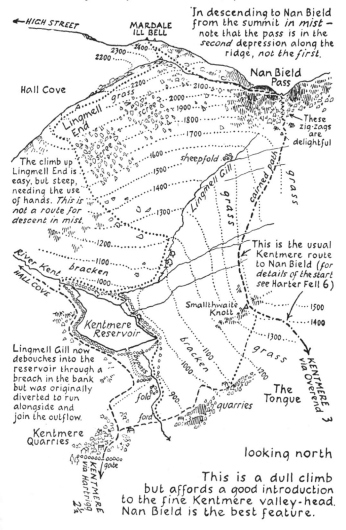

←HIGH STREET

MARDALE ILL BELL

In descending to Nan Bield from the summit *in mist* — note that the pass is in the *second* depression along the ridge, *not the first.*

2300
2400
2200

Nan Bield Pass

Hall Cove

Lingmell End

grass

2200

2100

2000

scree

1900

1800

scree

1700

1600

scree

sheepfold

1500

1400

1300

These zig-zags are delightful

Lingmell Gill

grass

cairned path

grass

The climb up Lingmell End is easy, but steep, needing the use of hands. *This is not a route for descent in mist.*

1200

River Kent

1100

HALL COVE

bracken

1000

This is the usual Kentmere route to Nan Bield (*for details of the start see Harter Fell 6*)

Smallthwaite Knott

1500

1400

Kentmere Reservoir

1300

bracken

grass

Lingmell Gill now debouches into the reservoir through a breach in the bank but was originally diverted to run alongside and join the outflow.

1100

1000

1200

KENTMERE via Overend 3

The Tongue

fold

900

ford

quarries

Kentmere Quarries

gate

KENTMERE via Hartrigg 2¼

looking north

This is a dull climb but affords a good introduction to the fine Kentmere valley-head. Nan Bield is the best feature.

THE SUMMIT

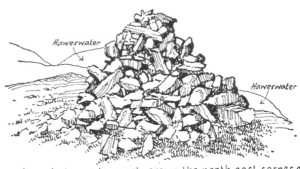

Haweswater

Haweswater

Two cairns, forty yards apart, crown the north-east corner of the undulating top, which is characterised by soft turf, patches of brown stones and occasional outcrops. There is nothing here to suggest the presence of fine crags close by, and a visit to them (north) adds interest to the summit.

DESCENTS : The usual way off is via Nan Bield Pass (the wall-shelter on the top of the pass is plainly visible from the summit cairn); to reach it, keep to the right of the direct line until a cairned path materialises. Both the north and east ridges are rough and the Lingmell End route is steep.

In mist, aim for Nan Bield Pass, noting that it crosses the second depression reached, not the first.

grass

HIGH STREET

grass

NORTH & EAST RIDGES

quartz boulders

NAN BIELD PASS

LINGMELL END

N

2400

100 yards

The stone shelters at Small Water

THE VIEW

Outstanding in the moderate view is the neighbouring ridge of Ill Bell, which, displaying its steep and rugged eastern face, looks magnificent from this angle. The long curve of High Street hides most of the western fells, and only the tips of the Bowfell group are visible above the rising skyline of Thornthwaite Crag.

Principal Fells

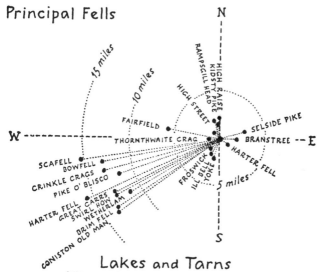

N

15 miles

10 miles

HIGH RAISE
KIDSTY PIKE
RAMPSGILL HEAD

HIGH STREET

FAIRFIELD

SELSIDE PIKE

W ---------------------------- E

THORNTHWAITE CRAG

BRANSTREE

SCAFELL

BOWFELL

HARTER FELL

CRINKLE CRAGS

PIKE O' BLISCO

FROSWICK

ILL BELL

YOKE

5 miles

HARTER FELL

GREAT CARRS

SWIRL HOW

WETHERLAM

BRIM FELL

CONISTON OLD MAN

S

Lakes and Tarns

NE and ENE: *Haweswater (two sections)*

Neither *Blea Water* nor *Small Water* can be seen from the cairn but both are worth the detour necessary to obtain bird's-eye views of them, the former from a break in the crags 100 yards north, the latter from above Piot Crag a quarter of a mile due east.

- -

The stone shelters at Small Water (illustration opposite)

Testimony to the former importance of Nan Bield Pass as a route for travellers and trade are the three shelters alongside the track where it crosses the bouldery shore of Small Water — erected for wayfarers overtaken by bad weather or darkness. These shelters are roughly but soundly built and roofed, but they are low and can be entered only by crawling. Once the body is insinuated snugly in their spider-infested recesses, however, the weather may be defied.

RIDGE ROUTES

To HIGH STREET, 2718': ⅘ mile : WNW then NW
Depression at 2350': 400 feet of ascent
An easy walk with interesting views

A sketchy path leaves the summit but is of little consequence; it is preferable to follow the edge of the escarpment after crossing the depression. At one point, marked by a cairn, there is a sensational downward view of Blea Water. In mist, incline west to the wall.

To THORNTHWAITE CRAG, 2569'
1⅓ miles : WNW, then WSW, W & NW
Depressions at 2350' and 2475'
250 feet of ascent

Easy walking, confusing in mist
When the short turf gives place to rough grass, keep the rising slope on the right hand and climb very slightly (*do not descend to left*). A track will be found as the end of the wall comes into sight.

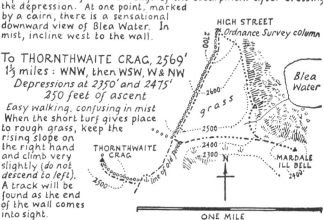

To HARTER FELL, 2539': 1 mile : SE. then ESE and E
Depression at 2100' (Nan Bield Pass) : 500 feet of ascent
A rough but interesting walk, with beautiful and impressive views

Aim first for the top of Nan Bield Pass (the wall-shelter there is in view from the summit), keeping to the right of the direct line until a cairned path to it is reached. Beyond the pass, an interesting ridge rises in rocky steps to the flat top of Harter Fell. In mist, the main difficulty will be in locating the Pass

Haweswater and Small Water
from the Nan Bield ridge

The summit crags

The Nab

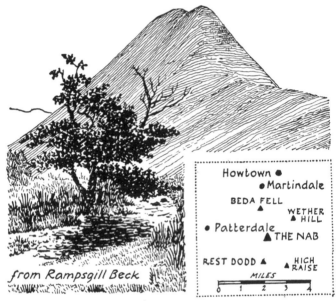

from Rampsgill Beck

Howtown ●
● Martindale
BEDA FELL
▲
WETHER ▲ HILL
● Patterdale
▲ THE NAB
REST DODD ▲
▲ HIGH RAISE

MILES

0   1   2   3   4

The Nab is situated wholly within the Martindale Deer Forest. The boundaries of the Forest are principally defined by the 'Forest Wall,' which encloses much of the Rampsgill and Bannerdale valleys and crosses the high ground between. This wall does not confine the deer — they roam freely beyond the boundaries — but it marks their home, their only safe refuge, their one sanctuary.

PLEASE DO NOT INTRUDE.

Red Deer Stag

NATURAL FEATURES

The Nab is, in character, akin to the three Dodds around Kirkstonefoot. Very steep-sided, soaring in symmetrical lines to a slender cone, it appears from the pastures of Martindale as a lofty wedge splitting the valley into two branches, Rampsgill and Bannerdale: from this viewpoint it may well be thought to be a separate and solitary fell. But in fact, as is seen from neighbouring heights, it is merely the butt of the northern shoulder of Rest Dodd. Its lower slopes are of bracken, its higher reaches of grass, with occasional scree on both flanks and a few rocks on Nab End. In addition to its other distinctions it has, on the wide ridge behind the summit, a most unpleasant morass of peat-hags, one of the worst in the district.

MAP

The only public right-of-way on this map is the valley road from Dalehead
The 1" Ordnance Survey Map shows three paths on The Nab
— these are PRIVATE stalkers paths.

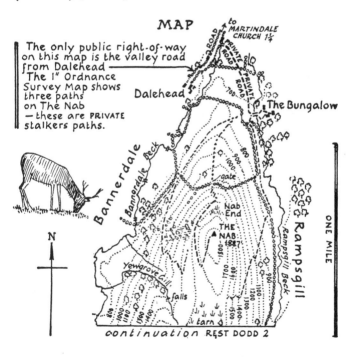

continuation REST DODD 2

ASCENTS

'Keep Out' notices, barricaded gates, and miles of barb wire must convey the impression even to the dullest-witted walker that there is no welcome here. That impression is correct. Wandering within the boundaries of the Deer Forest is not encouraged. Permission to visit the area should be sought at the keeper's Bungalow, and, justifiably, may not be granted.

The author carried out his explorations surreptitiously, and without permission (not caring to risk a refusal): he was not detected, but this may possibly have been due to his marked resemblance to an old stag, and other trespassers must not expect the same good fortune. Walkers in general should keep away. The keen 'peak-bagger' who is 'collecting' summits over 1886' must settle the matter with his conscience, and, if he decides he cannot omit The Nab, he may best approach it unobtrusively (but with permission) by way of the ridge from Rest Dodd, returning the same way. The following notes on direct ascents will therefore be of little interest to anybody but deer with a poor sense of direction.

The natural route of ascent is from Martindale. The three stalkers paths are distinct where they have been cut into the fellside, but the origins of the central and westerly paths in the lower enclosure (to which access is both barred and barbed) have largely vanished. The central route is most direct although the path becomes clear only beyond the gate in the cross-wall at 1300', and it has the advantage (which the others have not) that it continues, with one sharp angle, to within a few paces of the summit-cairn.

THE SUMMIT

The summit, a shapely dome, is completely grassy. A few stones have been carried up and make an untidy cairn.

The top of the central path is found within twenty yards on the west side of the cairn. It leads first south-west, away from its destination.

THE VIEW

Principal Fells

The view is 'open' only to the north. The most interesting feature, however, is the snug fit of Scafell Pike in the frame of Deepdale Hause

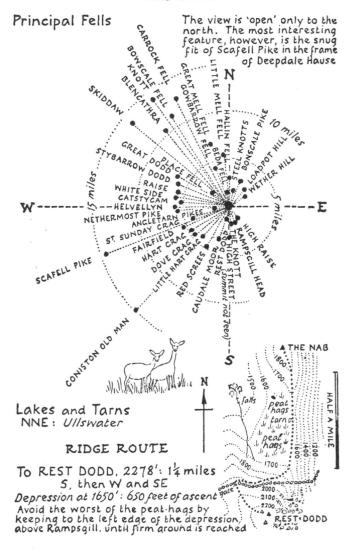

CARROCK FELL
BOWSCALE FELL
KNOTT
BLENCATHRA
GREAT MELL FELL
GOWBARROW FELL
LITTLE MELL FELL
SKIDDAW
N
HALLIN FELL
STEEL KNOTTS
BONSCALE PIKE
10 miles
LOADPOT HILL
WETHER HILL
GREAT DODD
STYBARROW DODD
PLACE FELL
BEDA FELL
RAISE
WHITE SIDE
CATSTYCAM
5 miles
HELVELLYN
NETHERMOST PIKE
ANGLETARN PIKES
W
E
5 miles
ST. SUNDAY CRAG
FAIRFIELD
HIGH RAISE
RAMPSGILL HEAD
HART CRAG
THE KNOTT
DOVE CRAG
HIGH STREET
LITTLE HART CRAG
REST DODD (summit not seen)
SCAFELL PIKE
RED SCREES
CAUDALE MOOR
RAMPSGILL HEAD
S
CONISTON OLD MAN

N

Lakes and Tarns
NNE: *Ullswater*

RIDGE ROUTE

To REST DODD, 2278': 1¼ miles
S, then W and SE
Depression at 1650': 650 feet of ascent
Avoid the worst of the peat-hags by keeping to the left edge of the depression above Rampsgill, until firm ground is reached

▲ THE NAB
1800
1700
1500
1600
falls
peat hags
tarn
peat hags
1600
1700
1800
HALF A MILE
1200
1400
gate
2000
2100
2200
▲ REST DODD

Place Fell

2154'

from Birks

Howtown •

▲ PLACE FELL

• Patterdale

MILES
0   1   2   3

Few fells are so well favoured as Place Fell for appraising neighbouring heights. It occupies an exceptionally good position in the curve of Ullswater, in the centre of a great bowl of hills; its summit commands a very beautiful and impressive panorama. On a first visit to Patterdale, Place Fell should be an early objective, for no other viewpoint gives such an appreciation of the design of this lovely corner of Lakeland.

NATURAL FEATURES

Place Fell rises steeply from the curve formed by the upper and middle reaches of Ullswater and its bulky mass dominates the head of the lake. Of only moderate elevation, and considerably overtopped by surrounding heights, nevertheless the fell more than holds its own even in such a goodly company: it has that distinctive blend of outline and rugged solidity characteristic of the true mountain. Many discoveries await those who explore: in particular the abrupt western flank, richly clothed with juniper and bracken and heather, and plunging down to the lake in a rough tumble of crag and scree, boulders and birches, is a paradise for the scrambler, while a more adventurous walker will find a keen enjoyment in tracing the many forgotten and overgrown paths across the fellside and in following the exciting and airy sheep-tracks that so skilfully contour the steep upper slopes below the hoary crest.

The eastern face, overlooking Boardale, is riven by deepcut gullies and is everywhere steep. Northward two ridges descend more gradually to the shores of Ullswater after passing over minor summits; from a lonely hollow between them issues the main stream on the fell, Scalehow Beck, which has good waterfalls. To the south, Boardale Hause is a well-known walkers' crossroads, and beyond this depression high ground continues to climb towards the principal watershed.

looking south

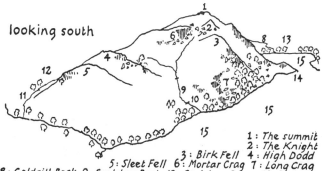

1 : The summit
2 : The Knight
3 : Birk Fell   4 : High Dodd
5 : Sleet Fell   6 : Mortar Crag   7 : Long Crag
8 : Goldrill Beck   9 : Scalehow Beck   10 : Scalehow Force   12 : Boardale
11 : Boardale Beck   13 : Patterdale   14 : Silver Point   15 : Ullswater

MAP

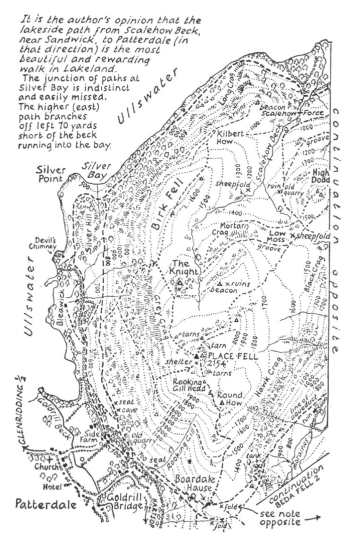

It is the author's opinion that the lakeside path from Scalehow Beck, near Sandwick, to Patterdale (in that direction) is the most beautiful and rewarding walk in Lakeland.
The junction of paths at Silver Bay is indistinct and easily missed.
The higher (east) path branches off left 70 yards short of the beck running into the bay.

Ullswater

Silver Point   Silver Bay

Devil's Chimney

Ullswater

Silver Hill

Birk Fell

Long Crag

Scalehow Force   beacon

Kilbert How

Scalehow beck

sheepfold   ruin old quarry

High Dodd

groove

Mortar Crag   Low Moss   sheepfold

groove

Bleawick

Grey Crag

The Knight

ruins   beacon

Black Crag

tarns   tarn

shelter

PLACE FELL 2154'

tarns

Hawk Crag

GLENRIDDING ½

Goldrill Beck

seat   cave

Rooking Gill Head

Round How

line of aqueduct   ruin

Side Farm

old quarry

seat

Rooking Gill

moraines

tank

Church

Hotel

Patterdale

Goldrill Bridge

Boardale Hause

fold

fold

SANDWICK 1

continuation opposite

continuation BEDA FELL 2

see note opposite →

MAP

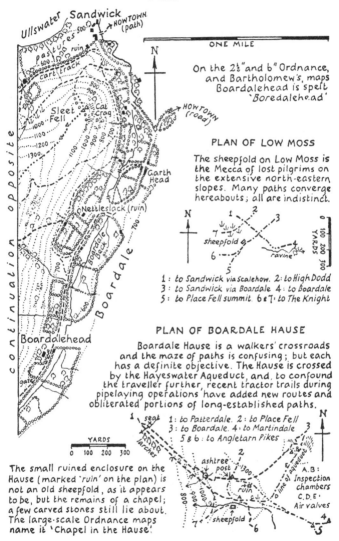

ONE MILE

On the 2½" and 6" Ordnance, and Bartholomew's, maps Boardalehead is spelt 'Boredalehead'

PLAN OF LOW MOSS

The sheepfold on Low Moss is the Mecca of lost pilgrims on the extensive north-eastern slopes. Many paths converge hereabouts; all are indistinct.

1: to Sandwick via Scalehow. 2: to High Dodd
3: to Sandwick via Boardale 4: to Boardale
5: to Place Fell summit. 6 & 7: to The Knight

PLAN OF BOARDALE HAUSE

Boardale Hause is a walkers' crossroads and the maze of paths is confusing; but each has a definite objective. The Hause is crossed by the Hayeswater Aqueduct, and, to confound the traveller further, recent tractor trails during pipelaying operations have added new routes and obliterated portions of long-established paths.

1: to Patterdale. 2: to Place Fell
3: to Boardale. 4: to Martindale
5 & 6: to Angletarn Pikes

A.B: Inspection chambers
C.D.E: Air valves

The small ruined enclosure on the Hause (marked 'ruin' on the plan) is not an old sheepfold, as it appears to be, but the remains of a chapel; a few carved stones still lie about. The large-scale Ordnance maps name it 'Chapel in the Hause'.

ASCENT FROM PATTERDALE
1700 feet of ascent : 1¼ miles

The face of Place Fell overlooking Patterdale is unremittingly and uncompromisingly steep, and the ascent is invariably made by way of the easier gradients of Boardale Hause, there being a continuous path on this route. (From the valley there appear to be paths going straight up the fell, but these are not paths at all : they are incipient streams and runnels).   As an alternative, an old neglected track that branches from the higher path to Silver Bay is recommended : this slants leftwards to the skyline depression between Birk Fell and Grey Crag, the easy remainder of the climb then following without the help of a path. This old track is difficult to locate from above and it is better not used for descent as there is rough ground in the vicinity.

looking north-north-east

The diversion of the old track from the higher path to Silver Bay is not distinct : it occurs a full half-mile beyond the quarry at a point where there is a bluff of grey rock on the left above some larches. A flat boulder marks the junction, and a few ancient cairns along the route are a help. Botanists will find much of interest here.
Note also, 200 yards up the old track, a faint path turning away on the right : this climbs high across the face below Grey Crag, is lost on scree, but can be traced beyond, on the 1500' contour, all the way to the usual route via Boardale Hause — an exhilarating high-level walk. From this path the summit may be gained without difficulty after leaving Grey Crag behind and crossing a small ravine.
On the Boardale Hause route, take the upper path at the fork near the seat. Watch for the zigzag : if this is missed the walker naturally gravitates to the lower path. The prominent ashtree is on the *upper* path.

One cannot sojourn at Patterdale without looking at Place Fell and one cannot look long at Place Fell without duly setting forth to climb it.   The time is very well spent.

ASCENT FROM SANDWICK
1700 feet of ascent : 2½ miles

An ascent direct from Boardale
may be made most easily
by the path leaving
the barn above
Nettleslack.

Five alternatives are
shown for the initial part
of the climb, the best on a
clear day being the pathless
route over the top of Sleet Fell
(which is steep). All ways converge
near the sheepfold on Low Moss,
beyond which is a further choice.

....

THE SUMMIT
A rocky ridge overtops gently-rising
slopes and has a cairn at one end and
a triangulation column at the other.
Many tarns adorn the top of the fell.
DESCENTS : Routes of descent are indicated in the illustration
of the view; that to Boardale Hause is safest in bad weather.

THE VIEW

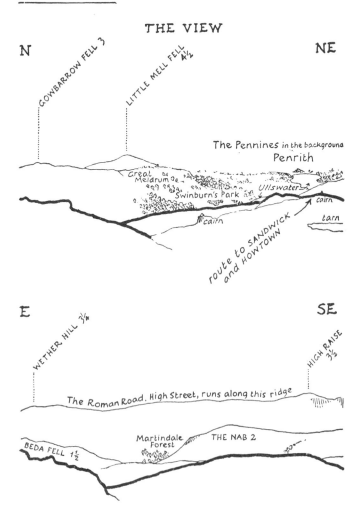

N   NE

GOWBARROW FELL 3

LITTLE MELL FELL 4½

The Pennines in the background

Penrith

Great Meldrum

Swinburn's Park

Ullswater

cairn

cairn

tarn

route to SANDWICK and HOWTOWN

E   SE

WETHER HILL 3¾

HIGH RAISE 3½

The Roman Road, High Street, runs along this ridge

Martindale Forest

THE NAB 2

BEDA FELL 1½

The thick line marks the visible boundaries
of Place Fell from the summit cairn.
  The figures following the names of fells
   indicate distances in miles.

THE VIEW

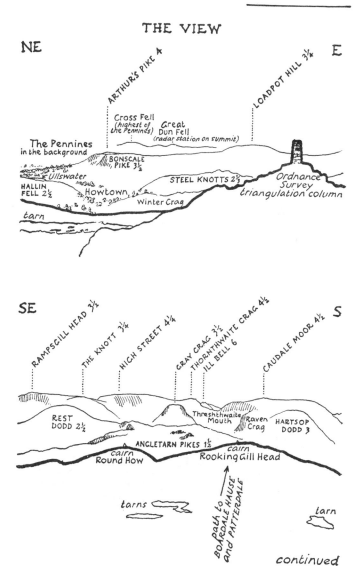

NE

ARTHUR'S PIKE 4

LOADPOT HILL 3¾   E

Cross Fell
(highest of
the Pennines)

Great
Dun Fell
(radar station on summit)

The Pennines
in the background

BONSCALE
PIKE 3½

Ullswater

HALLIN
FELL 2½

Howtown

Winter Crag

STEEL KNOTTS 2½

Ordnance
Survey
triangulation column

tarn

SE

RAMPSGILL HEAD 3½

THE KNOTT 3¼

HIGH STREET 4¼

GRAY CRAG 3½
THORNTHWAITE CRAG 4½
Ill Bell 6

CAUDALE MOOR 4½   S

REST
DODD 2½

Threshthwaite
Mouth

Raven
Crag

HARTSOP
DODD 3

ANGLETARN PIKES 1½

cairn
Round How

cairn
Rooking Gill Head

tarns

tarn

Path to
BOARDALE HAUSE
and PATTERDALE

continued

THE VIEW

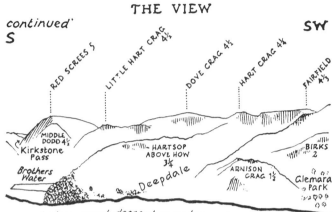

continued
S

SW

RED SCREES 5
LITTLE HART CRAG 4½
DOVE CRAG 4½
HART CRAG 4½
FAIRFIELD 4½

MIDDLE DODD 4½
Kirkstone Pass
Brothers Water
HARTSOP ABOVE HOW 3¼
Deepdale
ARNISON CRAG 1½
BIRKS 2
Glemara Park

*A steep, rough descent may be made to Patterdale
over this edge, but there is no path. The Boardale
Hause route is to be preferred, and takes no longer*

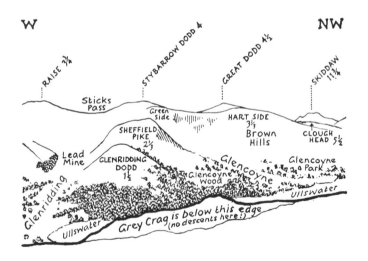

W

NW

RAISE 3¾
STYBARROW DODD 4
GREAT DODD 4½
SKIDDAW 11¾

Sticks Pass
Green side
HART SIDE 3½
Brown Hills
CLOUGH HEAD 5½

SHEFFIELD PIKE 2⅓
Lead Mine
GLENRIDDING DODD 1½
Glencoyne Wood
Glencoyne
Glencoyne Park

Glenridding
Ullswater
Ullswater

*Grey Crag is below this edge
(no descents here!)*

THE VIEW

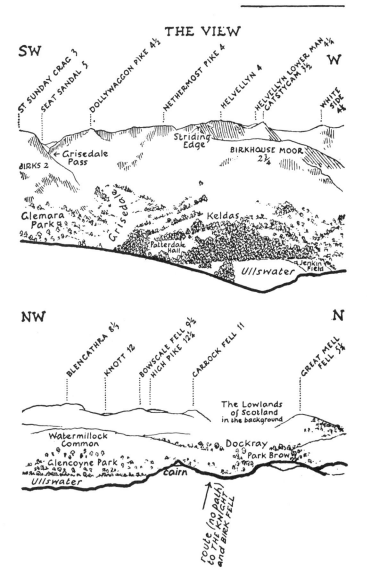

SW

ST. SUNDAY CRAG 3
SEAT SANDAL 5
DOLLYWAGGON PIKE 4½
NETHERMOST PIKE 4
HELVELLYN 4
HELVELLYN LOWER MAN 4¼
CATSTYCAM 3½
WHITE SIDE 4½

W

← Grisedale Pass
BIRKS 2
Striding Edge
BIRKHOUSE MOOR 2¼

Glemara Park
Grisedale
Keldas
Patterdale Hall
Jenkin Field
Ullswater

NW

BLENCATHRA 8⅓
KNOTT 12
BOWSCALE FELL 9½
HIGH PIKE 12½
CARROCK FELL 11
GREAT MELL FELL 5¼

N

The Lowlands of Scotland in the background

Watermillock Common
Dockray
Park Brow
Glencoyne Park
cairn
Ullswater

route (no path) TO THE KNIGHT and BIRK FELL

Rampsgill Head

2581'

Spelt 'Ramsgill Head' on
the Ordnance Survey maps.
Local writers include the 'p'

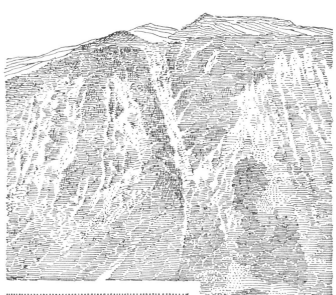

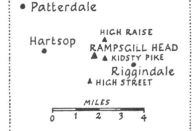

- Patterdale

Hartsop

HIGH RAISE ▲

RAMPSGILL HEAD
▲   ▲ KIDSTY PIKE

Riggindale ●

▲ HIGH STREET

MILES

0   1   2   3   4

from Gray Crag

NATURAL FEATURES

There is usually little difficulty in defining the boundaries of a mountain. If it rises in isolation there is no difficulty, and even if it is merely a high point on a ridge invariably its main slopes go down to valley-level, probably on both flanks, and the limit of its extent in other directions is, as a rule, marked by watercourses falling from the cols or depressions linking it with adjacent heights. Rampsgill Head is, geographically, a 'key' point in the High Street range, for two independent ridges of some importance leave its summit, and it is, therefore, all the more remarkable that a neat and precise definition of its natural boundaries cannot be given, largely because lower secondary summits on the side ridges are also regarded as separate fells and claim to themselves territory that would otherwise be attributed to the parent fell. It is also unusual for so prominent a height to be without an official name. Rampsgill Head is properly the name of the semicircle of high ground enclosing the rough upper reaches of the valley of Rampsgill but is now generally attached to all the fell above and beyond, although occasionally some writers have remedied the lack of a common title by referring to the whole mass hereabouts, east of the watershed, as Kidsty Pike, but this is incorrect.

The most impressive natural feature is the fringe of crags breaking abruptly at the edge of the summit facing Rampsgill, and the long slopes of boulder debris and scree below are an indication that, before the age of decay, the rock-scenery here must have been very striking. Grass predominates elsewhere but there is another steep face of rock, Twopenny Crag, falling into Riggindale. Hayeswater lies at the foot of the western slope, but the principal becks from the fell act as feeders of Ullswater and Haweswater.

Twopenny Crag

This fine arête (here seen from the south) starts from a leaning pinnacle on the west face and leads directly to the top of the fell. It is littered with loose rock and is obviously in a state of decay; otherwise it would surely deserve the attention of rock·climbers

The summit crags

The eastern aspect of the arête, here illustrated, reveals a prominent vertical buttress of sound, 'clean' rock, not of great height but perhaps worth carrying a rope up from Patterdale or Hartsop

MAP

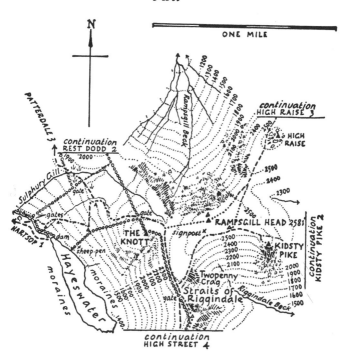

ONE MILE

N

PATTERDALE 3

continuation
REST DODD 2

Sulphury Gill

gate

gates

HARTSOP 1

dam

sheep-pen

Hayeswater

moraines

moraines

THE KNOTT

Rampsgill Beck

continuation
HIGH RAISE 3

HIGH RAISE

signpost

RAMPSGILL HEAD 2581

KIDSTY PIKE

continuation
KIDSTY PIKE 2

Twopenny Crag

Straits of Riggindale

Riggindale Beck

gate

continuation
HIGH STREET 4

The crags above the north-west face

ASCENTS FROM PATTERDALE AND HARTSOP
2200 feet of ascent : 4½ miles from Patterdale
2050 feet of ascent : 2¼ miles from Hartsop

The brief view down
Bannerdale from
Satura Crag is often
missed. Detour left
of the path to see it.

The valley down on
the right is that of
Hayeswater Gill : it
descends to Hartsop.

For a diagram of the
path from Hartsop
see The Knott 3

For a diagram of the ascent
to Angle Tarn from Patterdale
see Angletarn Pikes 5

looking east

 This is a most enjoyable excursion with a succession
of widely differing views, all excellent ; and the route
itself, never very distinct, is an interesting puzzle to
unravel. In bad weather, however, there will be some
difficulty, and a stranger may run into trouble on top
of Rampsgill Head, where there are crags.

ASCENT FROM MARDALE
1950 feet of ascent : 3½ miles from the road end

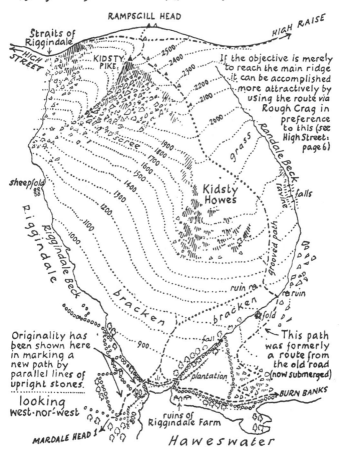

RAMPSGILL HEAD

Straits of Rigindale

HIGH STREET

HIGH RAISE

KIDSTY PIKE

2500
2400
2300
2200
2100
2000

If the objective is merely to reach the main ridge it can be accomplished more attractively by using the route via Rough Crag in preference to this (see High Street: page 6)

scree

1900
1800
1700
1600
1500
1400
1300
1200
1100
1000
900

Randale Beck ravine

grass

falls

Kidsty Howes

sheepfold

Rigindale Beck

Rigindale

grooved path

bracken

ruin

ruin

fold

bracken

Originality has been shown here in marking a new path by parallel lines of upright stones.

This path was formerly a route from the old road (now submerged)

looking west-nor'-west

fall

plantation

BURN BANKS

MARDALE HEAD

ruins of Rigindale Farm

Haweswater

This is a dull climb over neglected and fading paths that the Haweswater project committed to lingering death. Tough grass grows on the fellsides where once both dalesfolk and visitors trod. The gaunt ruins of Rigindale are symbolic of this dying route.

THE SUMMIT

MARDALE ILL BELL   HIGH STREET   THORNTHWAITE CRAG

On the right sort of day, the top is a pleasant place to linger awhile. The turf is delightful, there is some outcropping rock to add interest, the rim of crags is worthy of a leisurely and detailed exploration, the views are good in all directions. A prominent, well-built cairn stands on the edge of the abrupt north-west face; thirty yards away is the highest cairn — an untidy heap of stones — and sixty yards further south-west is a spectral signpost that once directed visitors to Mardale and Patterdale but lost its arms long ago: in any case its usefulness would be largely past, for few now go to Mardale.

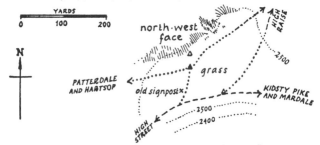

DESCENTS: For Patterdale and Hartsop, aim for The Knott to join the path there. For Mardale, use the ridge beyond Kidsty Pike — but the warning cannot be given too often until all old maps are out of circulation that Mardale Head is uninhabited, and the only beds in the valley are at the Haweswater Hotel on the far side of the lake.

In mist, the edge of the escarpment is sufficiently defined to give direction: keep it on the right hand if bound for either Patterdale or Hartsop and descend easy ground to the path. For Mardale, if the path over Kidsty Pike cannot be located, incline left and follow Randale Beck down to the valley.

RIDGE ROUTES

To HIGH RAISE, 2634' : ¾ mile : NE
Depression at 2450': 190 feet of ascent
Follow the edge of the crags north-east
(noting the arête on the way) and join a
narrow path (the old High Street) that
crosses the depression and continues
up the easy grass slope of High Raise
opposite. When the stony top is
reached leave the path and
pick a way among embedded
boulders to the cairn.

To THE KNOTT, 2423' : ⅓ mile : W
Depression at 2360'
65 feet of ascent
Descend the easy west slope to
the wall-corner in the depression
(the good path *crossed* here is the
regular Patterdale to High Street
route). He is tired indeed who
cannot gain the summit of The Knott from the corner of the wall, and
two minutes for the ascent is a generous time allowance.

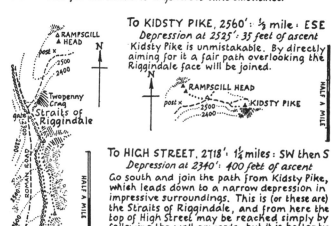

To KIDSTY PIKE, 2560' : ⅓ mile : ESE
Depression at 2525': 35 feet of ascent
Kidsty Pike is unmistakable. By directly
aiming for it a fair path overlooking the
Riggindale face will be joined.

To HIGH STREET, 2718', 1¼ miles : SW then S
Depression at 2340': 400 feet of ascent
Go south and join the path from Kidsty Pike,
which leads down to a narrow depression in
impressive surroundings. This is (or these are)
the Straits of Riggindale, and from here the
top of High Street may be reached simply by
following the wall onwards, but it is better by
far to arrive there by skirting the edge of the
cliffs on the left, which gives striking views.

All these routes are easy, and, with care, safe in mist

THE VIEW

Although the Helvellyn range conceals most of the western fells the view is very extensive and interesting. There is a commanding prospect of Rampsgill from the larger cairn.

Principal Fells

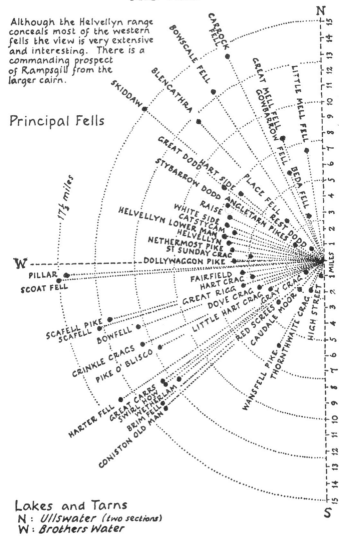

N

CARROCK FELL
BOWSCALE FELL
GREAT MELL FELL
GOWBARROW FELL
LITTLE MELL FELL
BLENCATHRA
SKIDDAW
BEDA FELL
GREAT DODD
HART SIDE
PLACE FELL
STYBARROW DODD
ANGLETARN PIKES
REST DODD
RAISE
WHITE SIDE
CATSTYCAM
HELVELLYN LOWER MAN
HELVELLYN
NETHERMOST PIKE
ST SUNDAY CRAG
DOLLYWAGGON PIKE

17½ miles

W

PILLAR
SCOAT FELL
FAIRFIELD
HART CRAG
GREAT RIGG
DOVE CRAG
GRAY CRAG
LITTLE HART CRAG
RED SCREES
CAUDALE MOOR
HIGH STREET
SCAFELL PIKE
SCAFELL
BOWFELL
CRINKLE CRAGS
PIKE O' BLISCO
WANSFELL PIKE
THORNTHWAITE CRAG
HARTER FELL
GREAT CARRS
SWIRL HOW
WETHERLAM
BRIM FELL
CONISTON OLD MAN

S

Lakes and Tarns
N : *Ullswater (two sections)*
W : *Brothers Water*

THE VIEW

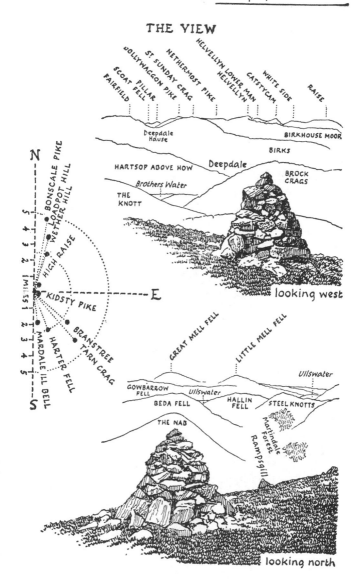

FAIRFIELD
SCOAT FELL
PILLAR
DOLLYWAGGON PIKE
ST SUNDAY PIKE
NETHERMOST CRAG
HELVELLYN LOWER MAN
HELVELLYN
CATSTYCAM
WHITE SIDE
RAISE

Deepdale Hause
BIRKHOUSE MOOR
BIRKS

HARTSOP ABOVE HOW
Deepdale
BROCK CRAGS

Brothers Water
THE KNOT

looking west

N

BONSCALE PIKE
LOADPOT HILL
WETHER HILL
HIGH RAISE

KIDSTY PIKE — E

BRANSTREE
HARTER FELL
TARN CRAG
MARDALE ILL BELL

S

GREAT MELL FELL
LITTLE MELL FELL
Ullswater

GOWBARROW FELL
Ullswater
HALLIN FELL
STEEL KNOTTS
BEDA FELL

THE NAB

Rampsgill
Martindale Forest

looking north

Rest Dodd

from Gray Crag

Howtown •
•
Martindale
▲ BEDA FELL
• Patterdale
ANGLETARN PIKES
▲ REST DODD
HIGH
Hartsop ▲ RAISE
•
▲ THE KNOTT
MILES
0   1   2   3   4

NATURAL FEATURES

The steep-sided ridge that divides Martindale into the secluded upper valleys of Bannerdale and Rampsgill, rises first to the shapely conical summit of The Nab and then more gradually to the rounded dome of Rest Dodd, which dominates both branches. It is a fell of little interest, although the east flank falls spectacularly in fans of colourful scree. Rest Dodd stands at an angle on the undulating grassy ridge coming down from the main watershed to the shores of Ullswater, and its south-west slope, which drains into Hayeswater Gill, is crossed by the track from Patterdale to High Street. Much of the fell is within the Martindale deer forest.

MAP

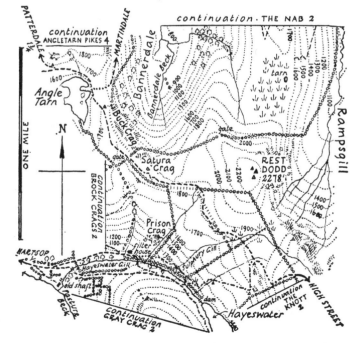

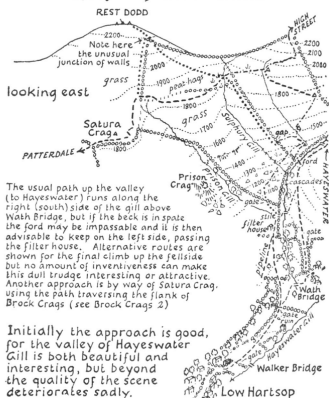

ASCENT FROM HARTSOP
1700 feet of ascent : 2 miles

REST DODD

looking east

Note here
the unusual
junction of walls

grass

peat hags

HIGH STREET

2200

2100

2000

1800

1500

Satura
Crag

grass

Sulphury Gill

gap

PATTERDALE

Prison
Crag

Prison Gill

ford

cascades

HAYESWATER

stile

filter
house

gate

pipeline

gate

Wath
Bridge

gate
ruin

gate

Hayeswater Gill

Walker Bridge

Low Hartsop

The usual path up the valley
(to Hayeswater) runs along the
right (south) side of the gill above
Wath Bridge, but if the beck is in spate
the ford may be impassable and it is then
advisable to keep on the left side, passing
the filter house. Alternative routes are
shown for the final climb up the fellside
but no amount of inventiveness can make
this dull trudge interesting or attractive.
Another approach is by way of Satura Crag,
using the path traversing the flank of
Brock Crags (see Brock Crags 2)

Initially the approach is good,
for the valley of Hayeswater
Gill is both beautiful and
interesting, but beyond
the quality of the scene
deteriorates sadly.

ASCENT FROM PATTERDALE
1900 feet of ascent : 3½ miles

Take the usual route to High Street (diagrams. Angletarn
Pikes 5 and High Street 5), which traverses the slopes of Rest
Dodd, but after crossing the top of Satura Crag, continue by
the wall directly ahead, bearing left at the top.
  (It is an interesting fact that the Patterdale-High Street route
formerly followed this wall up to its top corner and down the south
slope of Rest Dodd, an extra 300 feet of climbing which the present
more direct path avoids. No traces remain of a path by the wall.)

THE SUMMIT

A summit-cairn with a flagpole! Such is Rest Dodd's distinction, but not even this brave decoration relieves the drabness of the top of the fell. There are three cairns and a natural obstacle in the shape of an eroded peat-hag on the grassy summit.

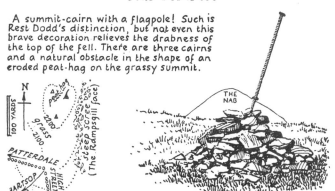

DESCENTS: Go down past the south cairn to the wall corner (or, more properly, the junction of two walls). Follow the wall west, and at its end will be found the path from High Street to Patterdale. Do not attempt any descents into Rampsgill, which is deer forest.

Buck Crag and Heck Crag from Satura Crag

THE VIEW

The view is neither so pleasing nor so extensive as that from The Knott nearby, although the full length of the Helvellyn range is well seen. The wild and lonely head of Rampsgill is an impressive sight. In the west, Great Gable fits snugly into the deep depression of Deepdale Hause.

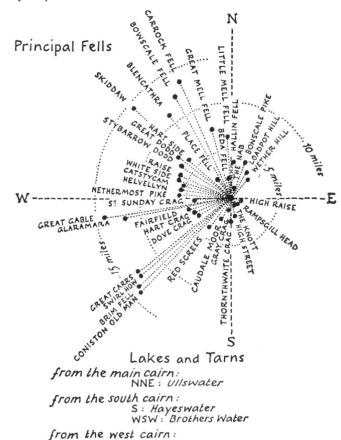

Principal Fells

Lakes and Tarns

from the main cairn:
NNE : Ullswater

from the south cairn:
S : Hayeswater
WSW : Brothers Water

from the west cairn:
NNE : Ullswater
WSW : Brothers Water
WNW : Angle Tarn

RIDGE ROUTES

To ANGLETARN PIKES, 1857': 1¾ miles: W, then NW
Depression at 1600': 300 feet of ascent

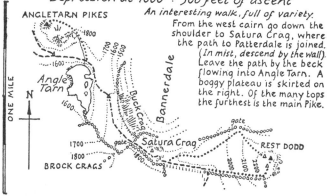

An interesting walk, full of variety.
From the west cairn go down the shoulder to Satura Crag, where the path to Patterdale is joined. (In mist, descend by the wall.) Leave the path by the beck flowing into Angle Tarn. A boggy plateau is skirted on the right. Of the many tops the furthest is the main Pike.

To THE KNOTT, 2423': ¾ mile: SSE
Depression at 1925': 500 feet of ascent
Merely a matter of following a wall.

From the south cairn the wall is soon reached (150 yards south). The depression is marshy. The High Street path is crossed at a gate.

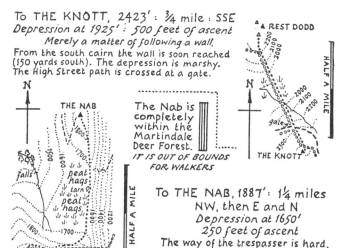

The Nab is completely within the Martindale Deer Forest.

IT IS OUT OF BOUNDS FOR WALKERS

To THE NAB, 1887': 1¼ miles
NW, then E and N
Depression at 1650'
250 feet of ascent
The way of the trespasser is hard, for this route is really unpleasant: the depression is a vast morass.

These notes and diagram are given only for the sake of completeness of records; no inducement to trespass is intended.

Sallows

better known locally
as Kentmere Park

from Badger Rock

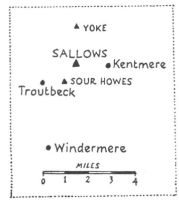

▲ YOKE

SALLOWS
▲   ● Kentmere

●   ▲ SOUR HOWES
Troutbeck

● Windermere

MILES
0   1   2   3   4

For most walkers, the fells
proper in this region start at
Garburn Pass and rise to the
north, but there are two hills,
twins almost, immediately to
the south of the Pass, worth a
mention although these are
not strictly walkers' territory.
The higher of the two is named
Sallows (on all maps), bounding
the Pass, and has much merit
as a viewpoint and a scantier
virtue as a grouse sanctuary.
It is not worth the detour for
anyone bound for Ill Bell and
places north, and, in any case,
there is not entirely free access
to the fell and visitors may be
requested to state their business

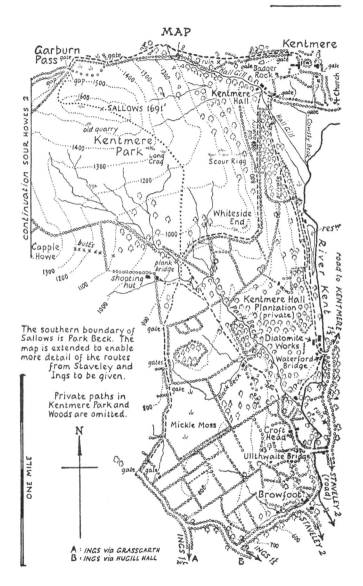

MAP

Garburn Pass

gate
gate
gap
gap
1400
1300
1500
600
× SALLOWS 1691'
old quarry
1400
Kentmere Park
1300
Long Crag
1200
continuation SOUR HOWES 2
Capple Howe
butts
×××××
×
1300
1200
1100
1000
shooting hut
plank bridge
900
gate
gates
gate
800
Mickle Moss
800
gate
gate

ruin ×
Hall Gill
Badger Rock
gate
Kentmere
gate
gate
Church
gate
Kentmere Hall
gate
Scour Rigg
Hall Gill
Cowsty Beck
Whiteside End
1000

River Kent
resr
road to KENTMERE 1½

Kentmere Hall Plantation (private)
Diatomite Works
Waterford Bridge
ruin
Black Beck
Park Beck
Croft Head
Ullthwaite Bridge
STAVELEY 2 (road)
Browfoot
600
700
800
STAVELEY 2

The southern boundary of Sallows is Park Beck. The map is extended to enable more detail of the routes from Staveley and Ings to be given.

Private paths in Kentmere Park and Woods are omitted.

ONE MILE

N

A : INGS via GRASSGARTH
B : INGS via HUGILL HALL

INGS 1½
A
B
INGS 1½

ASCENTS

The summit may be most easily and quickly visited from the top of Garburn Pass, where a gateway in the wall (without a gate, but barricaded) gives access to the fell. Alternatively it can be gained by a mile-long ascent from the Ings-Kentmere Hall bridle-path: a simple gradient, but not easy walking.

Sallows is not, as it appears to be, a 'short cut' to Garburn Pass from the south. Apart from doubts as to trespass, its tough heather slopes compel slow progress, and time will be lost. Garburn is best reached by orthodox routes.

THE SUMMIT

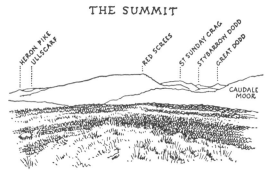

A curious curving mound of shale and grass, thirty feet long and narrow as a parapet, marks the highest part of the fell: it seems to be man-made, but is more probably a natural formation. It has no cairn. Heather and coarse grass cover the top of the fell, but there are small outcrops of rock west of the summit.

The summit mound

THE VIEW

The Lakeland scene occupies only half the panorama: it is outstandingly good to the west but unattractive northwards where Yoke fills much of the horizon. The rest of the view is exceedingly extensive, varied and interesting, covering a wide area from the Pennines across Morecambe Bay to Black Combe.

Principal Fells

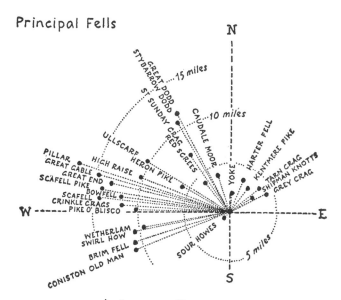

Lakes and Tarns : SSW : *Windermere*

Sallows from Ullthwaite Bridge

Haweswater Hotel
●

● Swindale Head

Mardale ▲ SELSIDE PIKE
Head ●

▲ BRANSTREE

▲ HARTER FELL

MILES
0   1   2   3   4

from Mosedale Beck
near the waterfalls

NATURAL FEATURES

One of the lesser-known fells is Selside Pike on the eastern fringe of the district, commanding the head of the shy and beautiful little valley of Swindale. Its neglect is scarcely merited, for although the summit is a dull grass mound with little reward in views the fell has an extremely rugged eastern face that closes the valley in dramatic fashion : here are dark crags, rarely-visited waterfalls, a curious dry tarn-bed set amongst moraines and, above.it, a perfect hanging valley, the two being connected by a very formidable gully.

For countless ages Selside Pike has looked down upon Swindale and seen there a picture of unspoiled charm. Now the engineers have taken over the valley — they may not spoil it, but it is more certain that they can not improve it. Swindale is almost the only remaining Lakeland valley that does not cater for the motorist. Please, Manchester, leave it as nearly as you found it!

Selside Pike
from the old
corpse-road

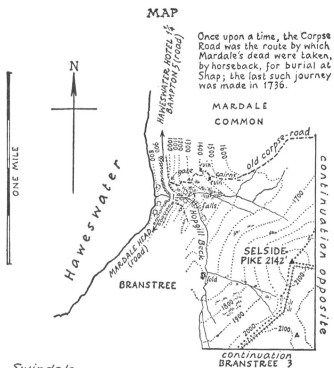

MAP

Once upon a time, the Corpse Road was the route by which Mardale's dead were taken, by horseback, for burial at Shap; the last such journey was made in 1736.

N

ONE MILE

HAWESWATER HOTEL 1½
BAMPTON 5 (road)

MARDALE COMMON

old corpse-road

HAWESWATER

continuation opposite

gate
ruin
cairns
ruin
falls

MARDALE HEAD (road)

Hopgill Beck

BRANSTREE

fold

SELSIDE PIKE 2142'

continuation
BRANSTREE 3

Swindale
with Selside Pike at the head of the valley

MAP

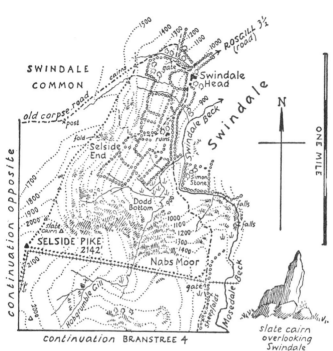

SWINDALE COMMON

1500
1400
1300
1200
1100
1000
ROSGILL 3½ (road)

cairn
gate
Swindale Head

old corpse road
post
fold
Selside End

900
Swindale Beck
Swindale

ruins

N

ONE MILE

Simons Stone

continuation opposite

1700
1800
1900
2000
slate cairn △
SELSIDE PIKE 2142'

Dodd Bottom
900
1000
1100
1200
1300
1400

falls
falls

Nabs Moor

2100
2000
△

Hobgrumble Gill

gate
steepfolds
Mosedale Beck

continuation BRANSTREE 4

slate cairn
overlooking
Swindale

Swindale Head

ASCENT FROM SWINDALE HEAD

1200 feet of ascent : 1½ miles (via the north-east ridge)
1350 feet of ascent : 2¼ miles (via the Mosedale path)

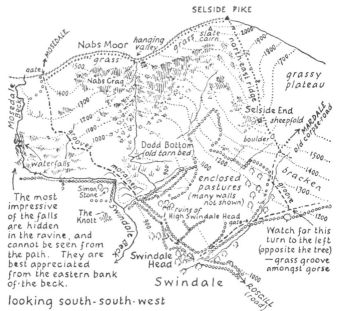

SELSIDE PIKE

MOSEDALE

Nabs Moor

hanging valley

grass

slate cairn

2000

1900

1800

north east ridge

1700

grassy plateau

gate

1500

grass

Nabs Crag

1400

1300

Selside End sheepfold

MARDALE old corpse road

1200

1100

cove

1000

Dodd Bottom (old tarn bed)

1500

1400

bracken

1300

Mosedale Beck

waterfalls

moraines

Simon Stone

1200

1100

enclosed pastures (many walls not shown)

boulder

groove

The Knott

Swindale Beck

ruins of High Swindale Head

gate

1200

The most impressive of the falls are hidden in the ravine, and cannot be seen from the path. They are best appreciated from the eastern bank of the beck.

Swindale Head

1000

Swindale

Watch for this turn to the left (opposite the tree) — grass groove amongst gorse

ROSGILL (road)

looking south-south-west

The quality of the scenery deteriorates when the tedious higher slopes are reached. If returning to Swindale, ascend by the ridge and descend by the wire fence, making a detour to see the waterfalls.

THE SUMMIT

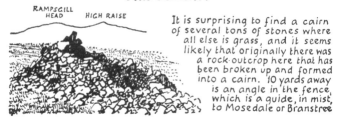

RAMPSGILL HEAD HIGH RAISE

It is surprising to find a cairn of several tons of stones where all else is grass, and it seems likely that originally there was a rock outcrop here that has been broken up and formed into a cairn. 10 yards away is an angle in the fence, which is a guide, in mist, to Mosedale or Branstree

THE VIEW

The view towards Lakeland is disappointing, being confined to the surroundings of Mardale except for a glimpse of distant fells over the Straits of Riggindale.
Eastwards, however, there is a splendid prospect of the Pennines, with Shap village prominent.

Principal Fells

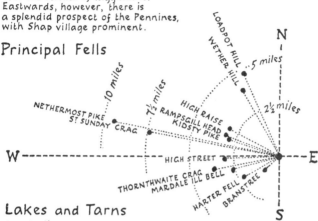

Lakes and Tarns

NNW : *Haweswater*
Small Water and *Blea Water* can both be seen by walking
   30 yards W in the direction of High Street.
And if *Swindale Reservoir* materialises, there will be an excellent
   full-length view of it from the slate cairn NE.

RIDGE ROUTE

To BRANSTREE, 2333' : 1½ miles : SW
Two shallow depressions : 450 feet of ascent
   An easy walk on grass ; safe in mist
   The only objects of interest on this dull trudge
are man-made : the old survey post and the
fine cairn on Artlecrag Pike. The 2209'
summit is hardly worth traversing
although it has (which the
main summits have not) a
view of Helvellyn. *In mist
keep to the fence.*

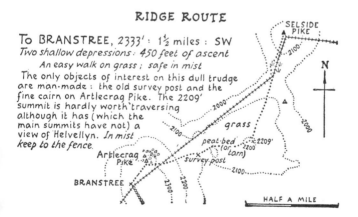

Shipman Knotts

from Stockdale

▲ HARTER FELL

KENTMERE   ▲ TARN
▲ PIKE   CRAG
▲
ILL BELL
                              GREY
SHIPMAN KNOTTS   CRAG

• Kentmere

Longsleddale •

0   1   2   3   4

Shipman Knotts is of moderate altitude and would have called for no more than the brief comment that it is a shoulder of Kentmere Pike had it not earned for itself a separate chapter by reason of the characteristic roughnesses of its surface. Rocky outcrops are everywhere on the steep slopes, persisting even in the woods of Sadgill, although these seldom attain the magnitude of crags. This fell is usually climbed on the way to Harter Fell from the south, and its rock should be welcomed for there is precious little beyond. The south slope carries the path from Kentmere to Lonasleddale

MAP

continuation KENTMERE PIKE 3

The cart-track linking Stile End and Sadgill is the regular highway between Kentmere and Longsleddale; a line of telegraph posts accompanies it. Highest point: 1120 feet.

ONE MILE

ASCENTS

from Kentmere : 1400 feet of ascent : 2¼ miles
from Sadgill : 1300 feet of ascent : 1½ miles

Shipman Knotts is usually climbed as a means of gaining access to the Harter Fell ridge, but is an interesting short expedition in itself. The ascent is most easily made alongside the wall running up from the summit of the Stile End-Sadgill 'pass'; but from Kentmere the ridge north of the fell-top may be reached by a grooved path leaving Hollowbank. Safe in mist if the wall route is followed.

The summit from the south

THE SUMMIT

KENTMERE PIKE

Three rocky knolls, on the east side of the wall, form the summit, and of these the middle one is highest. It is without a cairn.

DESCENTS : Cross the wall and follow it south to the pass, where turn left for Longsleddale, right for Kentmere. In mist, this is a safe route

The summit-ridge from Goat Scar

THE VIEW

The northern half of the panorama is restricted to nearby heights of greater elevation; the southern is open, extensive and pleasing. There is a good view of Longsleddale.

Principal Fells

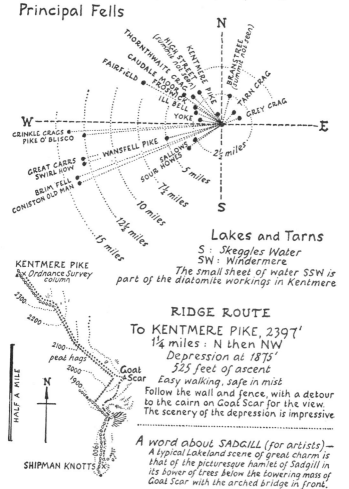

Lakes and Tarns

S : Skeggles Water
SW : Windermere
The small sheet of water SSW is part of the diatomite workings in Kentmere

RIDGE ROUTE

To KENTMERE PIKE, 2397'

1¼ miles : N then NW
Depression at 1875'
525 feet of ascent
Easy walking, safe in mist
Follow the wall and fence, with a detour to the cairn on Goat Scar for the view.
The scenery of the depression is impressive.

A word about SADGILL (for artists) —
A typical Lakeland scene of great charm is that of the picturesque hamlet of Sadgill in its bower of trees below the towering mass of Goat Scar with the arched bridge in front.

Sour Howes

better known locally as
Applethwaite Common

from Troutbeck

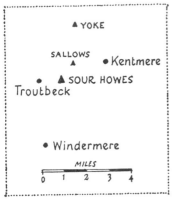

▲ YOKE

SALLOWS
▲   • Kentmere

•   ▲ SOUR HOWES
Troutbeck

• Windermere

MILES

0   1   2   3   4

Although all maps agree that
the summit of this fell is named
Sour Howes, its broadest flank,
carrying the Garburn Pass Road
down to Troutbeck, is far better
known as Applethwaite Common;
this flank is traversed also by
the pleasant Dubbs Road. There
is little about the fell to attract
walkers, and nothing to justify
a detour from the main Ill Bell
ridge to the north, for although
the views are really good they
are better from the main ridge.
There is heather on the eastern
slopes, and therefore, inevitably,
grouse; and therefore, inevitably,
shooting butts: one may admire
the construction of these butts
while deploring their purpose.

MAP

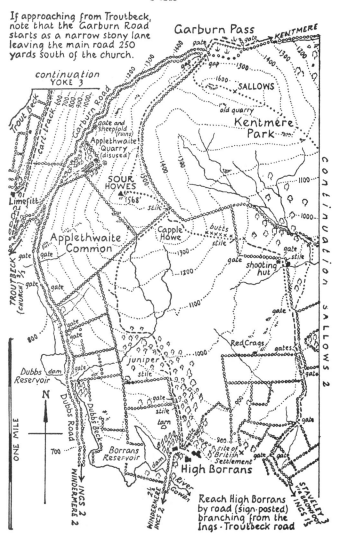

If approaching from Troutbeck, note that the Garburn Road starts as a narrow stony lane leaving the main road 250 yards south of the church.

continuation YOKE 3

Troutbeck

cart-track

Garburn Road

Limefitt

Garburn Pass

KENTMERE

gate

gap

gate

gap

SALLOWS

old quarry

Kentmere Park

gate and sheepfold (ruins)

Applethwaite Quarry (disused)

SOUR HOWES ▲ 1568

stile

Applethwaite Common

gate

gate

gate

gate

Capple Howe

butts

stile

gate

stile

gate

shooting hut

gate

continuation SALLOWS 2

TROUTBECK (CHURCH) 3/4

gate

gate

gate

gate

Red Crags

gates

gate

juniper

stile

gate

tarn

gate

Dubbs Reservoir

dam

N

ONE MILE

Dubbs Road

Dubbs Beck

Borrans Reservoir

dam

Borrans Reservoir

High Borrans

site of British Settlement

gate

gate

River Gowan

WINDERMERE 2 1/4
INGS 2

INGS 2

STAVELEY 2 1/4
BROWFOOT
INGS 1 1/2

Reach High Borrans by road (sign-posted) branching from the Ings-Troutbeck road

ASCENTS

Sour Howes is a fell with no obvious appeal to walkers, and few other than conscientious guide-book writers will visit its summit; nevertheless it makes a pleasant walk from Windermere, Ings or Staveley, especially on a clear day for the views are good.

Two lanes leave Ings (one *via* Grassgarth and one *via* Hugill Hall) and another leaves Browfoot (two miles up the Kentmere valley from Staveley): these join, and at the terminus the old bridle-path to Kentmere Hall may be followed for a mile, when it may be forsaken and a way made to the top by the shooting-butts, using the stiles to cross the walls.

An enchanting path leaves High Borrans, climbing first through juniper bushes, then bracken, then heather; when it peters out keep to the route shown on the map.

The summit is easily visited from the top of Garburn Pass: here a gap in the wall (a gateway without a gate) gives access to the enclosure containing the highest point.

THE SUMMIT

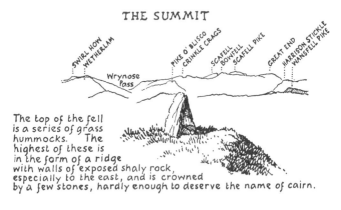

The top of the fell is a series of grass hummocks. The highest of these is in the form of a ridge with walls of exposed shaly rock, especially to the east, and is crowned by a few stones, hardly enough to deserve the name of cairn.

Red Screes from Sour Howes

THE VIEW

The crowded skyline in the west arrests the attention, with the vertical profile of Scafell above Mickledore prominent in the scene. Langdale Pikes are well seen between and below Great End and Great Gable. There is a very extensive and beautiful prospect southwards from the far Pennines round to Morecambe Bay and Black Combe.

Principal Fells

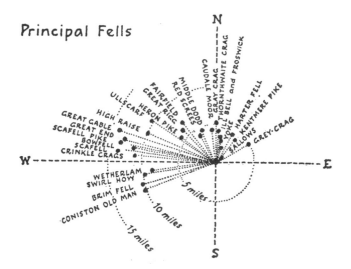

GREAT GABLE
GREAT END
SCAFELL PIKE
BOWFELL
SCAFELL
CRINKLE CRAGS
HIGH RAISE
ULLSCARF
FAIRFIELD
GREAT RIGG
HERON PIKE
RED SCREES
MIDDLE DODD
DOVE CRAG
CAUDALE
THORNTHWAITE CRAG
ILL BELL and FROSWICK
YOKE
HARTER FELL
KENTMERE PIKE
SALLOWS
GREY CRAG
WETHERLAM
SWIRL HOW
BRIM FELL
CONISTON OLD MAN

N
W — E
S

5 miles
10 miles
15 miles

Lakes and Tarns
S: *Borrans Reservoir*
SSW: *Windermere*

Most old and disused quarries are gloomy and repellant places but Applethwaite Quarry, near the Garburn Road, is relieved from desolation by a planting of conifers and a magnificent view. An interesting feature is the old weighbridge, now overgrown. A favourite with foxes, this quarry!

Applethwaite Quarry

Steel Knotts

1414'

summit named Pikeawassa

from Howe Grain Beck

Wether Hill's western flank swells into a bulge, Gowk Hill, which itself sends out a crooked bony arm northwards to form a lofty independent ridge running parallel to the main range and enclosing with it the short hidden valley of Fusedale. On the crest of this ridge, rock is never far from the surface and it breaks through in several places, notably at the highest point, which is a craggy tor that would worthily embellish the summit of many a higher fell. This freakish gnarled ridge is Steel Knotts; the summit-tor is named, on the best of authority, (but not by many, one imagines) Pikeawassa. (O.S. 1" and 2½"map.)

Howtown
●
STEEL KNOTTS
▲   ▲ LOADPOT
              HILL
          ▲ WETHER HILL

MILES

0   1   2   3

MAP

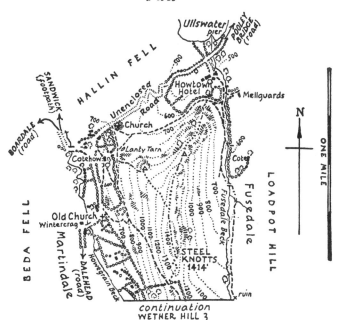

continuation
WETHER HILL 3

ASCENTS

FROM HOWTOWN : The natural route of ascent is by the craggy ridge above Howtown. This has an intimidating aspect but it is without perils and gives an exhilarating scramble. Leave the path at its base by a concrete waterworks notice inscribed thus : and climb upwards between the rocks ; initially there is a track obscured by bracken. A cairn surmounts the steepest part of the ridge and the walking is then easy to the top of the fell.

FROM LANTY TARN : A pronounced shoulder, with two tiers of crag, descends north-west to Lanty Tarn and offers a less satisfactory route. From the tarn (a shallow pond) climb to the right (south) of the crags to a cairn above them. An easy slope then follows.

FROM MARTINDALE OLD CHURCH : This is the easiest way. Climb the fellside by the church to a good path slanting upwards (this is the Martindale path to the High Street range). Leave the path at a wall and turn up left to the ridge and again left to the top.

Although Steel Knotts is of small extent and modest elevation, it should not be climbed in mist. If caught by mist on the top, descend south to the wall and return by the path to Martindale Old Church.

THE SUMMIT

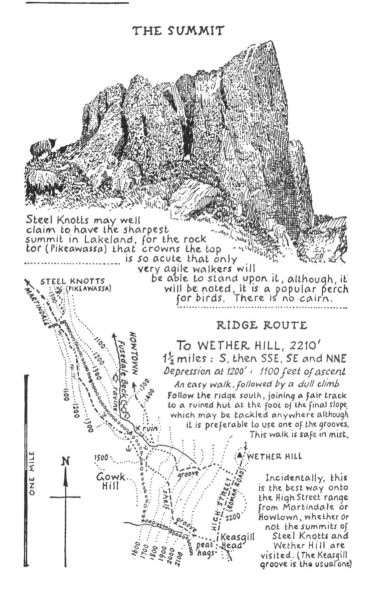

Steel Knotts may well claim to have the sharpest summit in Lakeland, for the rock tor (Pikeawassa) that crowns the top is so acute that only very agile walkers will be able to stand upon it, although, it will be noted, it is a popular perch for birds. There is no cairn.

RIDGE ROUTE

To WETHER HILL, 2210'

1½ miles : S, then SSE, SE and NNE
Depression at 1200' : 1100 feet of ascent

An easy walk, followed by a dull climb

Follow the ridge south, joining a fair track to a ruined hut at the foot of the final slope, which may be tackled anywhere although it is preferable to use one of the grooves. This walk is safe in mist.

Incidentally, this is the best way onto the High Street range from Martindale or Howtown, whether or not the summits of Steel Knotts and Wether Hill are visited. (The Keasgill groove is the usual one)

THE VIEW

Principal Fells

This is the best viewpoint for the upper Martindale district, the highlight of a charming scene being the confluence of the remote Rampsgill and Bannerdale valleys

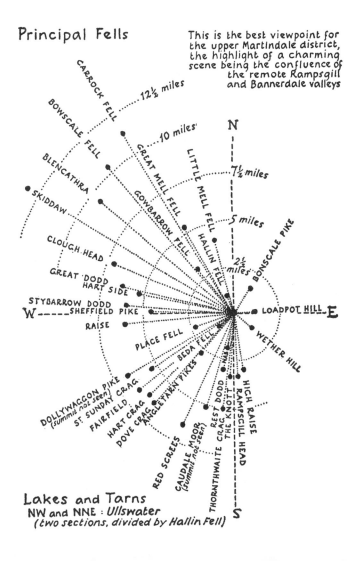

CARROCK FELL
BOWSCALE FELL
BLENCATHRA
SKIDDAW
GREAT MELL FELL
GOWBARROW FELL
LITTLE MELL FELL
HALLIN FELL
BONSCALE PIKE
CLOUGH HEAD
GREAT DODD
HART SIDE
STYBARROW DODD
SHEFFIELD PIKE
RAISE
LOADPOT HILL
PLACE FELL
WETHER HILL
BEDA FELL
DOLLYWAGGON PIKE (summit not seen)
ST. SUNDAY CRAG
FAIRFIELD
HART CRAG
DOVE CRAG
ANGLETARN PIKES
NAB
HIGH RAISE
REST DODD
THE KNOTT
RAMPSGILL HEAD
RED SCREES
CAUDALE MOOR (summit not seen)
THORNTHWAITE CRAG

12½ miles
10 miles
7½ miles
5 miles
2½ miles

N
W
E
S

Lakes and Tarns

NW and NNE : *Ullswater*
(two sections, divided by Hallin Fell)

Tarn Crag

2176'

Shap •

• Swindale Head

Mardale
Head •   • Wet
        ▲ BRANSTREE   Sleddale

▲ HARTER FELL

▲   ▲ TARN CRAG
KENTMERE
PIKE   ▲ GREY CRAG

                                road
                                summit

        Longsleddale •

MILES
0   1   2   3   4   5

from Sadgill Wood

NATURAL FEATURES

The gradually rising wall of fells bounding Longsleddale
on the east reaches its greatest elevation, and its terminus,
in Tarn Crag. To the valley this fell presents a bold front,
with Buckbarrow Crag a conspicuous object, but on other
sides it is uninteresting, especially eastwards where easy
slopes merge into the desolate plateaux of Shap Fells. It
is enclosed on the north by the wide, shallow depression
of Mosedale, a natural pass linking Longsleddale with
Swindale in wild and lonely surroundings: here a solitary
shepherd's cottage merely accentuates the utter dreariness
of the scene. (Yet on rare occasions of soft evening light
even Mosedale can look inexpressibly beautiful!). The
walker hereabouts will be in no doubt, without reference to
his map, that he has passed outside the verge of Lakeland.

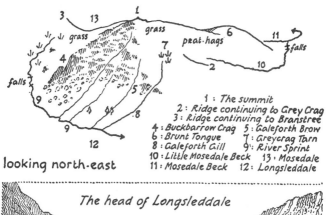

1 : The summit
2 : Ridge continuing to Grey Crag
3 : Ridge continuing to Branstree
4 : Buckbarrow Crag   5 : Galeforth Brow
6 : Brunt Tongue   7 : Greycrag Tarn
8 : Galeforth Gill   9 : River Sprint
10 : Little Mosedale Beck   13 : Mosedale
11 : Mosedale Beck   12 : Longsleddale

looking north-east

The head of Longsleddale

Tarn Crag 3

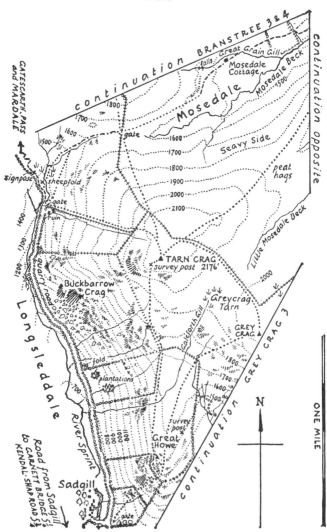

MAP

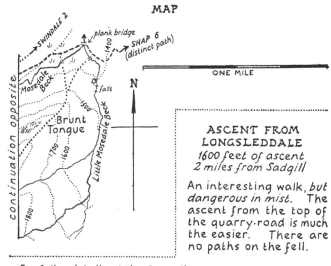

SWINDALE 2

plank bridge

SHAP 6
(distinct path)

1400

Mosedale Beck

↑ falls

continuation opposite

1500

Brunt Tongue

1700

1600

Little Mosedale Beck

1800

N

ONE MILE

ASCENT FROM LONGSLEDDALE
1600 feet of ascent
2 miles from Sadgill

An interesting walk, *but dangerous in mist.* The ascent from the top of the quarry-road is much the easier. There are no paths on the fell.

For fuller details of the Great Howe route, see GREY CRAG 4

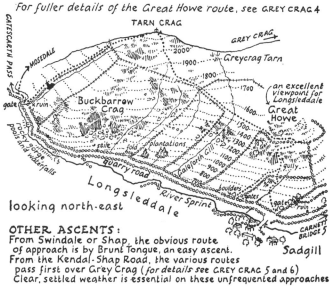

TARN CRAG

GREY CRAG

MOSEDALE

GATESCARTH PASS

Greycrag Tarn

2000

1900

1800

1700

an excellent viewpoint for Longsleddale

gate

ruin

Buckbarrow Crag

Great Howe

1600

rocky gorge
pools and waterfalls

stile

fold

plantations

Galeforth Gill

1500
1400
1300
1200
1100
1000
900
800
700

gully

quarry road

River Sprint

boulders

gates

gate

ruin

Longsleddale

GARNETT BRIDGE 5

looking north-east

Sadgill

OTHER ASCENTS:
From Swindale or Shap, the obvious route of approach is by Brunt Tongue, an easy ascent.
From the Kendal-Shap Road, the various routes pass first over Grey Crag (*for details see* GREY CRAG 5 *and* 6)
Clear, settled weather is essential on these unfrequented approaches

THE SUMMIT

Not until Manchester Corporation's engineers climbed Tarn Crag, in the course of their duty, and departed from it for the last time, did its summit acquire distinction: the wide dreary top then found itself left with a curious structure — a high wooden platform with a core of stone and concrete, which served for a time as a survey post during the construction of the Longsleddale tunnel conveying the Haweswater Aqueduct south. Now, thirty years later, the aqueduct is in place and the scars are gone from the valley — but the hoary survey post still stands, defying the weather and puzzling the few travellers who come this way and find no clue as to its purpose.

The highest part of the fell, marked by a small undistinguished cairn, is a hundred yards away, to the east.

DESCENTS : The routes of ascent should be used for descent.

In mist, keep strictly to the fences. Crags obstruct the direct way down into Longsleddale. Eastwards, Shap Fells are a wilderness to avoid in bad weather.

THE VIEW

Anyone who climbs Tarn Crag for a view of Lakeland will be very disappointed, for, excepting the Coniston fells, nothing is to be seen of the distant west because of the adjacent heights across the deep trench of Longsleddale. On a clear day there is ample recompense, however, in the excellent panorama from east round to south — where, for a hundred miles, the noble skyline of the Pennines and the wide seascape of Morecambe Bay present themselves to view without obstruction.

Principal Fells

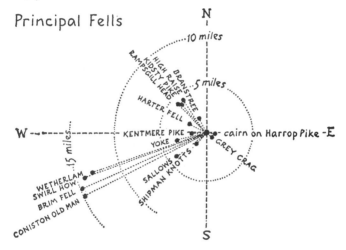

Lakes and Tarns: SW · Windermere

Kentmere Pike across Longsleddale

RIDGE ROUTES

To BRANSTREE, 2333′ : 1¾ miles : N, then NW
Depression at 1650′: 700 feet of ascent
Rough grass, but easy gradients; safe in mist
This is a long, featureless walk: interest is confined to the views of Longsleddale and Harter Fell. Traces of a cart-track may indicate the route taken up the easy slope of Tarn Crag for the transport of material when the survey post was under construction. Keep to the left of the wall on Branstree for the best views, to the right of it for shelter from rain.

To GREY CRAG, 2093′
¾ mile : NE, then SE and S
Depression at 1940′:
170 feet of ascent
An easy walk, best accomplished by following the fence across the depression to avoid the marsh that masquerades as Greycrag Tarn. In mist, Grey Crag is better left alone.

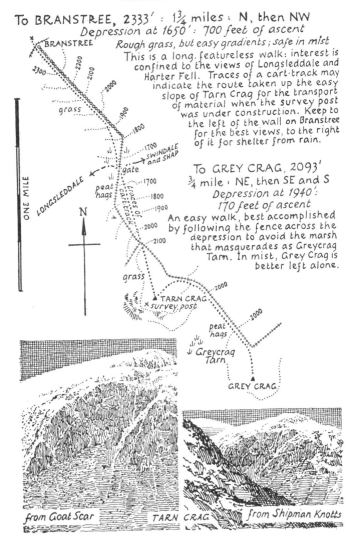

from Goat Scar TARN CRAG *from Shipman Knotts*

Buckbarrow Crag

Thornthwaite Crag 2569'

Hartsop

HIGH
STREET

CAUDALE
MOOR

THORNTHWAITE
CRAG

ILL BELL

Kentmere

Troutbeck

MILES

0 1 2 3 4

from Caudale Moor

NATURAL FEATURES

Occupying a commanding position overlooking four valleys, Thornthwaite Crag is one of the better-known fells east of Kirkstone, owing not a little of its fame to its tall pillar of stones, a landmark for miles around. Its name derives from the long shattered cliff facing west above the upper Troutbeck valley; there are also crags fringing the head of Hayeswater Gill and above the early meanderings of the River Kent. Apart from these roughnesses the fell is grassy, the ground to the east of the summit forming a wide plateau before rising gently to the parent height of High Street, of which Thornthwaite Crag is a subsidiary; it has, however, a ridge in its own right, this being a narrow steep-sided shoulder that ends in Gray Crag, northwards. Streams flow in three directions: north to Ullswater, south to Windermere and south-east along the Kentmere valley.

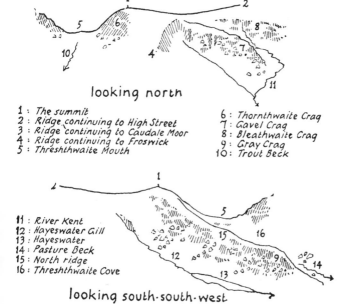

looking north

1 : The summit
2 : Ridge continuing to High Street
3 : Ridge continuing to Caudale Moor
4 : Ridge continuing to Froswick
5 : Threshthwaite Mouth

6 : Thornthwaite Crag
7 : Gavel Crag
8 : Bleathwaite Crag
9 : Gray Crag
10 : Trout Beck

11 : River Kent
12 : Hayeswater Gill
13 : Hayeswater
14 : Pasture Beck
15 : North ridge
16 : Threshthwaite Cove

looking south-south-west

MAP

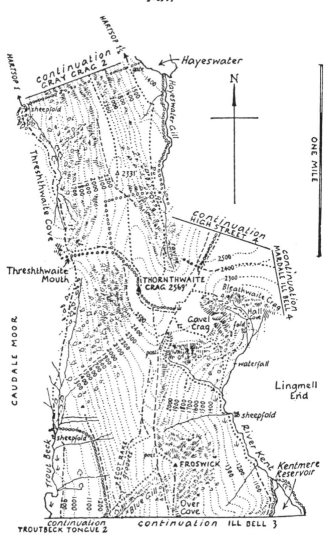

ASCENT FROM HARTSOP
2000 feet of ascent : 3¾ miles

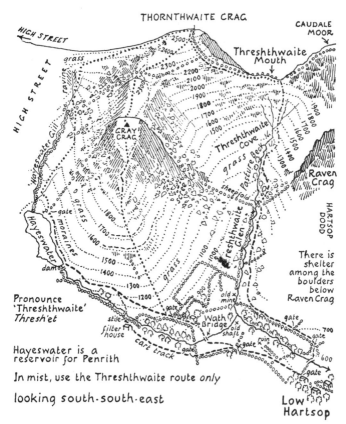

Pronounce
'Threshthwaite'
Thresh'et

Hayeswater is a
reservoir for Penrith

In mist, use the Threshthwaite route only

looking south-south-east

This is a very interesting and enjoyable expedition.
Of the three routes illustrated, that via Hayeswater
starts well but has a tame and tiring conclusion. If
the return is to be made to Hartsop, Threshthwaite
is the best approach, the descent being made along
the north ridge over Gray Crag, which itself has an
airy situation and good views.

ASCENT FROM TROUTBECK
2200 feet of ascent
5 miles via Scot Rake; 5½ via Threshthwaite Mouth

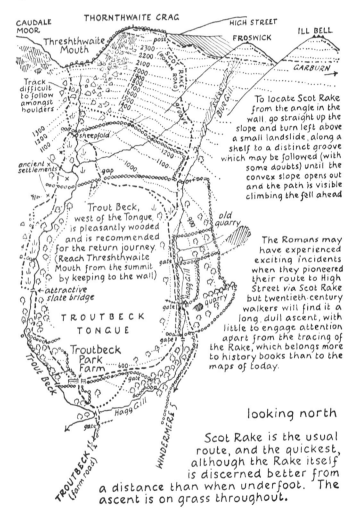

To locate Scot Rake from the angle in the wall, go straight up the slope and turn left above a small landslide, along a shelf to a distinct groove which may be followed (with some doubts) until the convex slope opens out and the path is visible climbing the fell ahead

The Romans may have experienced exciting incidents when they pioneered their route to High Street via Scot Rake but twentieth-century walkers will find it a long, dull ascent, with little to engage attention apart from the tracing of the Rake, which belongs more to history books than to the maps of today.

Trout Beck, west of the Tongue, is pleasantly wooded and is recommended for the return journey. (Reach Threshthwaite Mouth from the summit by keeping to the wall)

looking north

Scot Rake is the usual route, and the quickest, although the Rake itself is discerned better from a distance than when underfoot. The ascent is on grass throughout.

ASCENT FROM KENTMERE RESERVOIR
1650 feet of ascent : 2 miles

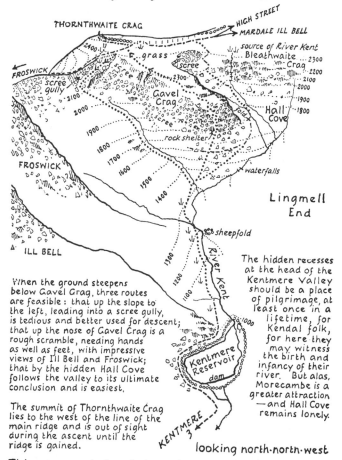

THORNTHWAITE CRAG

HIGH STREET

MARDALE ILL BELL

2400

E. grass

source of River Kent

Bleathwaite Crag

2300

FROSWICK

scree gully

2100

2000

2300

Gavel Crag

2200

2100

2000

1900

Hall Cove

1800

1900

scree

1800

1700

rock shelter

1600

FROSWICK

1500

waterfalls

1400

Lingmell End

ILL BELL

1300

sheepfold

1200

River Kent

1100

When the ground steepens below Gavel Crag, three routes are feasible: that up the slope to the left, leading into a scree gully, is tedious and better used for descent; that up the nose of Gavel Crag is a rough scramble, needing hands as well as feet, with impressive views of Ill Bell and Froswick; that by the hidden Hall Cove follows the valley to its ultimate conclusion and is easiest.

The summit of Thornthwaite Crag lies to the west of the line of the main ridge and is out of sight during the ascent until the ridge is gained.

1000

Kentmere Reservoir

dam

KENTMERE 3

The hidden recesses at the head of the Kentmere Valley should be a place of pilgrimage, at least once in a lifetime, for Kendal folk, for here they may witness the birth and infancy of their river. But alas, Morecambe is a greater attraction — and Hall Cove remains lonely.

looking north·north·west

This approach leads into the unfrequented dalehead of Kentmere and abounds in interest and variety all the way from the village. Rainsborrow Crag, up on the left, is a tremendous object en route, and Ill Bell and Froswick reveal themselves most effectively.

THE SUMMIT

Thornthwaite
Beacon

It is sometimes difficult to recall
the details of familiar summits
but surely all who have climbed
Thornthwaite Crag will identify
it in memory by its remarkable
14-feet column, one of the most
distinctive cairns in Lakeland.
It stands in the angle of a wall
that traverses the summit. A
few outcrops of flaky rock in
the vicinity relieve the general
grassiness of the top of the fell.
DESCENTS: In clear weather
all the routes of ascent may be
reversed, but that to Kentmere
via Gavel Crag is not suggested
nor should routes be 'invented'
as there is rough ground about.
In bad conditions, descend
to Troutbeck or Hartsop *via*
Threshthwaite Mouth —to
which the wall leads when
followed north-west. For
Kentmere, go to the end of
the wall eastwards; here
turn right along a faint
path for 200 yards to
a scree gully on the
left, which descend.

looking north to
Ullswater

Threshthwaite Mouth

looking south to
Windermere

THE VIEW

Principal Fells

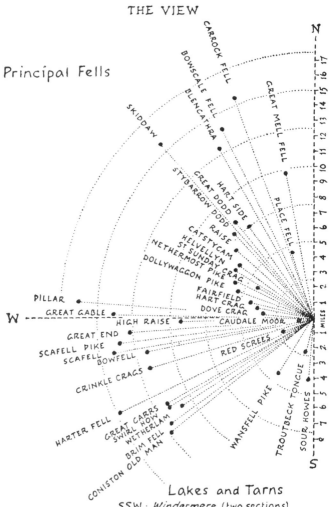

Lakes and Tarns

SSW : *Windermere* (two sections)
NNW : The upper reach of *Ullswater* may
be seen by descending the west slope for 50 yards, or by following
the wall north.   N : *Hayeswater* is brought into view by a
short walk (130 yards) in the direction of High Street.

THE VIEW

The tall column, the wall, and adjacent high ground northwards between them interrupt the panorama — and various 'stations' must be visited to see all there is to see. The view is good, but not amongst the best; the northern prospect, in particular, is best surveyed from the slope going down to Threshthwaite Mouth.

The best feature in the scene is Windermere, to which the Troutbeck valley leads the eye with excellent effect.

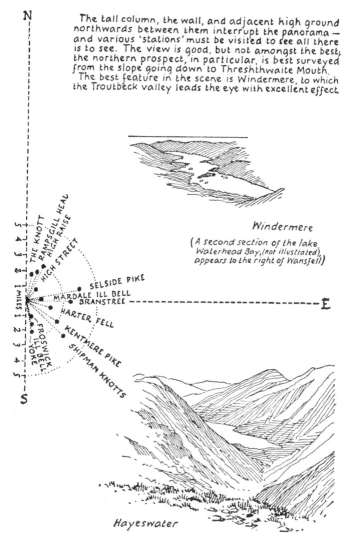

Windermere

(A second section of the lake, Waterhead Bay, (not illustrated), appears to the right of Wansfell)

Hayeswater

RIDGE ROUTES

To CAUDALE MOOR, 2502': 1 mile: NW, W and WSW
Depression at 1950': 560 feet of ascent
A rough scramble, made safe in mist by walls

There is more to this walk than appears at first sight, for the gap of Threshthwaite Mouth is deep and it links slopes that are steep and rough. Keep by the wall until the broken crag of Caudale is left behind. The Caudale flank above the gap can be dangerous when the rocks are iced or under snow.

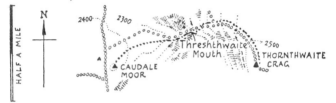

To GRAY CRAG, 2286': 1¼ miles: slightly W of N
Two minor depressions: 150 feet of ascent
An easy, interesting walk, better avoided in mist.

Straightforward walking along the descending and narrowing north ridge leads first to the nameless conical height of point 2331', then to the flat top of Gray Crag. Two broken walls are crossed en route. Both flanks are heavily scarped and dangerous in mist.

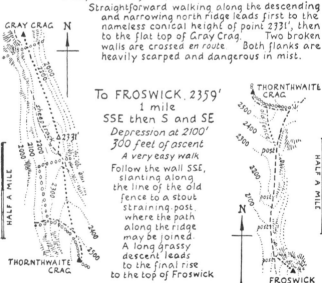

To FROSWICK, 2359'
1 mile
SSE then S and SE
Depression at 2100'
300 feet of ascent
A very easy walk

Follow the wall SSE, slanting along the line of the old fence to a stout straining post, where the path along the ridge may be joined. A long grassy descent leads to the final rise to the top of Froswick

RIDGE ROUTES

To HIGH STREET, 2718' : 1¼ miles : SE, then E and NE
Depression at 2475' : 250 feet of ascent
A very simple walk, safe in mist

Follow the wall to its eastern terminus, avoid the bog there, and continue along the line of an old fence to join another wall that runs directly to and beyond the top of High Street. All is grass.

To MARDALE ILL BELL, 2496'
1⅓ miles : SE, then E, ENE and ESE
Depressions at 2475' and 2350' : 200 feet of ascent
Easy walking, but a confusing area in mist

Leave the corner of the High Street wall by a plain track trending eastwards and when this becomes indistinct keep on over long grass in the same direction, descending slightly to the depression ahead. In mist, take care not to descend to the right into Hall Cove.

Thornthwaite Crag
from the south ridge of
Caudale Moor

Troutbeck Tongue

properly named
The Tongue, Troutbeck Park

from the Kirkstone-Windermere road

▲ CAUDALE MOOR

▲ ILL BELL

TROUTBECK ▲
TONGUE

● Troutbeck

MILES
0 1 2 3

There are many Tongues in Lakeland, all of them wedges of high or rising ground between enclosing becks that join below at the tip, but none is more distinctive or aptly named than that in the middle of the Troutbeck Valley. Other Tongues usually have their roots high on a mountainside, but this one thrusts forward from the floor of the dalehead. Although of very modest altitude, it has an attraction for the gentler pedestrian as a viewpoint for the valley, and makes an admirable short excursion in pleasant scenery from Windermere or Troutbeck or, by Skelghyll Woods, from Ambleside.

MAP

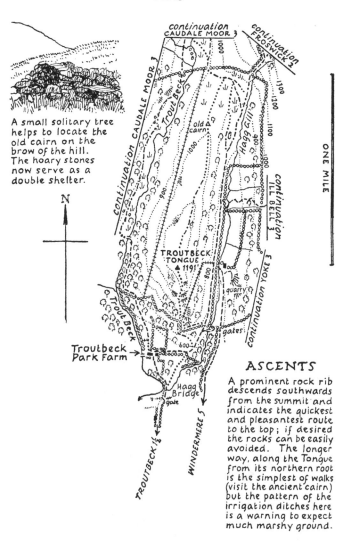

A small solitary tree helps to locate the old cairn on the brow of the hill. The hoary stones now serve as a double shelter.

N

ONE MILE

continuation CAUDALE MOOR 3

continuation FROSWICK 2

continuation CAUDALE MOOR 3

Troutbeck

Trout Beck

Hagg Gill

old cairn

continuation ILL BELL 3

continuation YOKE 3

TROUTBECK TONGUE ▲ 1191'

quarry

gates

Troutbeck Park Farm

Hagg Bridge

gate

Trout Beck

TROUTBECK 1½

WINDERMERE 5

ASCENTS

A prominent rock rib descends southwards from the summit and indicates the quickest and pleasantest route to the top; if desired the rocks can be easily avoided. The longer way, along the Tongue from its northern root is the simplest of walks (visit the ancient cairn) but the pattern of the irrigation ditches here is a warning to expect much marshy ground.

THE SUMMIT

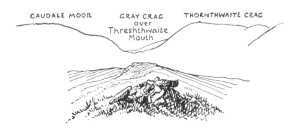

CAUDALE MOOR   GRAY CRAG over Threshthwaite Mouth   THORNTHWAITE CRAG

The rocky scramble up the south ridge from the cart-track is entertaining enough to hold out the promise of a summit equally interesting, but the promise is not fulfilled by the reality, which is a grassy knoll a little higher than several more nearby, and graced by a small heap of stones. Apart from the view down the valley to Windermere, nothing here is worth comment.

Slate bridge, Trout Beck

THE VIEW

Troutbeck Tongue is set deep
in the bottom of a great bowl
of hills, all of which overtop it
and limit the scene. Only to the
south is there an open view —
of Windermere — but there is
also a peep of distant fells
to the west.

Principal Fells

SCAFELL PIKE
W - - - - - - BOWFELL - E

CRINKLE CRAGS
PIKE O' BLISCO

Hart Crag (Caudale Moor)
RED SCREES
CAUDALE MOOR
GRAY CRAG
THORNTHWAITE CRAG
FROSWICK
ILL BELL
YOKE
SALLOWS
SOUR HOWES
WANSFELL
Dodd Hill (Wansfell)

N
E
S

5 miles
2½ miles
10 miles

Lakes and Tarns

SSW : *Windermere*
(middle and lower reaches)

Windermere and the Troutbeck Valley

CAUDALE
▲ MOOR
▲
RED SCREES

▲ WANSFELL
● Ambleside

● Troutbeck

MILES
0   1   2   3

from High Grove

NATURAL FEATURES

Caudale Moor sends out three distinct ridges to the south, and the most westerly and longest of the three descends to a wide depression (crossed by the Kirkstone road) before rising and narrowing along an undulating spur that finally falls to the shores of Windermere. This spur is Wansfell, and, although its summit-ridge is fairly narrow and well-defined, the slopes on most sides are extensive, the fell as a whole occupying a broad tract of territory between Ambleside and the Troutbeck valley. Except northwards, the lower slopes are attractively wooded; the upper reaches are mainly grassy, but at the south-west extremity of the ridge there is a rocky bluff known as Wansfell Pike, which is commonly but incorrectly regarded as the top of the fell. Other crags masked by trees, flank the Kirkstone road at Troutbeck and Jenkins Crag in Skelghyll Woods is a very popular viewpoint. The main streams flow from marshy ground east of the ridge — this was the scene of the cloudburst in June 1953 and these the gentle becks that suddenly became raging torrents and caused so much damage in the Troutbeck district.

MAP

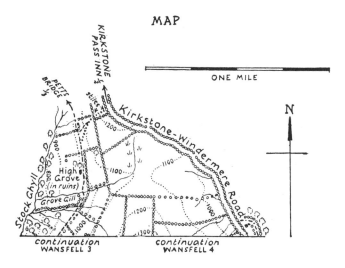

MAP

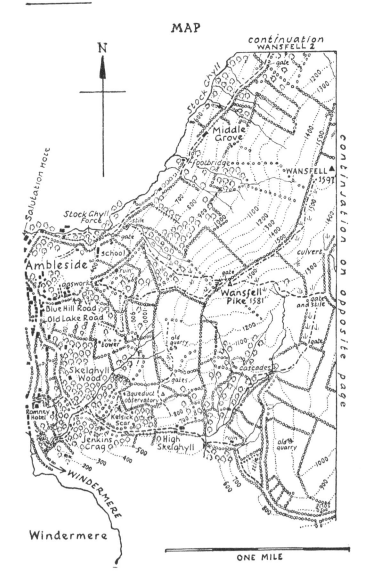

continuation
WANSFELL 2

continuation on opposite page

N

Salutation Hotel

Stock Ghyll

Middle
Grove

footbridge

WANSFELL
1597

Stock Ghyll Force

stile

gate

school

ruin

1200

1300

1400

1500

1600

1700

culvert

1300

Ambleside

gasworks

gate

Wansfell
Pike 1581

gate
and stile

Blue Hill Road

Old Lake Road

1200

gate

tower

old
quarry

1100

Skelghyll
Wood

gates

cascades

aqueduct
observatory

Romney
Hotel

Kelsick Scar

800

700

Jenkins
Crag

High
Skelghyll

ruin

old
quarry

1000

500

400

300

200

700

WINDERMERE

600

800

900

Windermere

ONE MILE

MAP

continuation WANSFELL 2

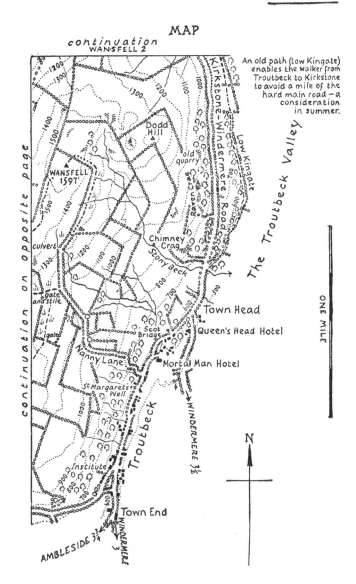

An old path (Low Kingate) enables the walker from Troutbeck to Kirkstone to avoid a mile of the hard main road — a consideration in summer.

The Troutbeck Valley

Kirkstone-Windermere Road

Low Kingate

Dodd Hill ▲

old quarry

Rough Crag

WANSFELL ▲ 1597'

Chimney Crag

Stony Beck

culvert

gate and stile

gate

Town Head

Queen's Head Hotel

Scot Bridge

Mortal Man Hotel

Nanny Lane

St Margaret's Well +

Troutbeck

WINDERMERE 3½

Institute

Town End

ONE MILE

N

AMBLESIDE 3¾   WINDERMERE 3

continuation on opposite page

ASCENT FROM AMBLESIDE
1500 feet of ascent : 2½ miles

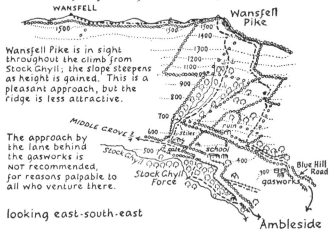

Wansfell Pike is in sight throughout the climb from Stock Ghyll; the slope steepens as height is gained. This is a pleasant approach, but the ridge is less attractive.

The approach by the lane behind the gasworks is NOT recommended, for reasons palpable to all who venture there.

looking east-south-east

ASCENT FROM TROUTBECK
1100 feet of ascent : 1¾ miles

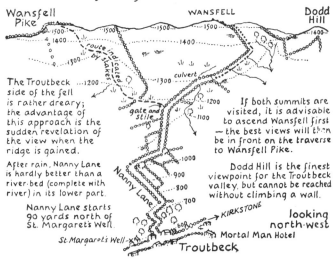

The Troutbeck side of the fell is rather dreary; the advantage of this approach is the sudden revelation of the view when the ridge is gained.

After rain, Nanny Lane is hardly better than a river-bed (complete with river) in its lower part.

Nanny Lane starts 90 yards north of St. Margaret's Well.

If both summits are visited, it is advisable to ascend Wansfell first — the best views will then be in front on the traverse to Wansfell Pike.

Dodd Hill is the finest viewpoint for the Troutbeck valley, but cannot be reached without climbing a wall.

looking north-west

THE SUMMIT

A grassy hummock, a little higher than many around, is the true summit of the fell: a few small stones confirm it. It is an unattractive place, rarely visited; better is the rocky top of Wansfell Pike, which at least is mildly interesting and unique in possessing an iron gate. The higher summit lies 150 yards east of the ridge-wall, which, in mist, is a safe guide as far as Wansfell Pike, whence paths go down to Ambleside (west) and Troutbeck (east).

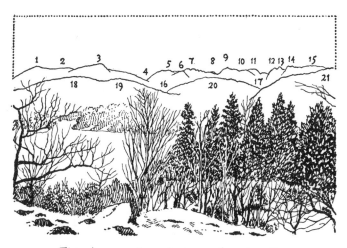

The view westwards from Jenkins Crag

1 : Coniston Old Man
2 : Brim Fell
3 : Wetherlam
4 : Wrynose Pass
5 : Cold Pike
6 : Pike o'Blisco
7 : Crinkle Crags
8 : Scafell
9 : Bowfell
10 : Esk Pike
11 : Great End
12 : Loft Crag
13 : Pike o'Stickle
14 : Harrison Stickle
15 : Pavey Ark
16 : Little Langdale
17 : Great Langdale
18 : Black Fell
19 : Park Fell
20 : Lingmoor Fell
21 : Loughrigg Fell

THE VIEW
FROM THE SUMMIT OF WANSFELL

As a viewpoint, the highest part of the summit is inferior to the lower Wansfell Pike, and, curiously, fewer fells can be seen. Nevertheless, the prospect westwards is very charming.

Principal Fells

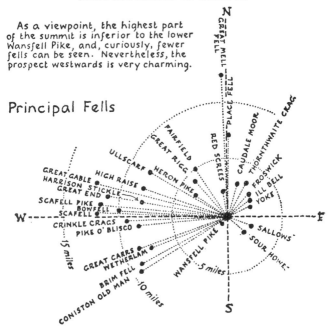

N

GREAT MELL FELL
PLACE FELL
FAIRFIELD
GREAT RIGG
RED SCREES
CAUDALE MOOR
THORNTHWAITE CRAG
ULLSCARF
HERON PIKE
FROSWICK
ILL BELL
GREAT GABLE
HIGH RAISE
YOKE
HARRISON STICKLE
GREAT END
SCAFELL PIKE
BOWFELL
SCAFELL
W — — — — *E*
CRINKLE CRAGS
PIKE O' BLISCO
SALLOWS
SOUR HOWE
GREAT CARRS
WETHERLAM
WANSFELL PIKE
BRIM FELL
5 miles
15 miles
10 miles
CONISTON OLD MAN
S

Lakes and Tarns

S : *Windermere*
WSW : *Little Langdale Tarn*
W : *Grasmere*
W : *Rydal Water*

Red Screes, from the summit

THE VIEW
FROM WANSFELL PIKE

Wansfell Pike excels in its view of Windermere, the graceful curve of the lake showing to great advantage. Westwards, the scene is especially beautiful.
Red Screes is a fine object in the north; the east is dull.

Principal Fells

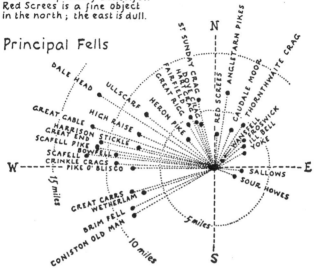

Lakes and Tarns

S : *Windermere*
SW : *Blelham Tarn*
W : *Little Langdale Tarn*
WNW : *Grasmere*
WNW : *Rydal Water*
The two sheets of water on the lower slopes of Sour Howes, southeast, are reservoirs.

Windermere, from Wansfell Pike

RIDGE ROUTE

To CAUDALE MOOR, 2502'
4½ miles : N, then NE and E
Depression at 1100'
1550 feet of ascent

A long, easy, uninteresting trudge.

Although this is the natural
high-level approach to the High
Street range from Ambleside, it
is not a regular walkers' route in
the section between Wansfell and
St. Raven's Edge, and awkward
walls have to be climbed that
were not built to be climbed.
On grass all the way. Safe
in mist, but marshy patches
will then prove unpleasant.

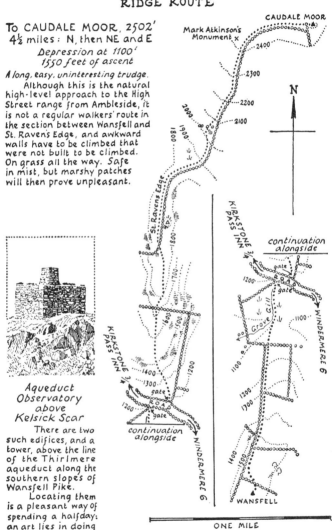

Aqueduct
Observatory
above
Kelsick Scar

There are two
such edifices, and a
tower, above the line
of the Thirlmere
aqueduct along the
southern slopes of
Wansfell Pike.

Locating them
is a pleasant way of
spending a halfday:
an art lies in doing
this *sans* wallscaling.

ONE MILE

Stock Ghyll Force

Wether Hill

spelt 'Weather' Hill
on Bartholomew's map

2210'
approx

from Beda Fell

Howtown

LOADPOT
▲ HILL

Bampton

▲ WETHER HILL

▲ HIGH RAISE

MILES
0 1 2 3 4

NATURAL FEATURES

The High Street range has largely lost its appeal to the walker by the time he reaches the twin grassy mounds of Wether Hill on the long tramp along its spine northwards, and there is nothing here to call for a halt. The top, scarcely higher than the general level of the ridge, is quite without interest, while the eastern slopes are little better although traversed by two good routes from Bampton; but the western flank, characteristically steeper, has the peculiarity of Gowk Hill, a subsidiary height which itself develops into a parallel ridge running north: this encloses, with the main ridge, the little hidden valley of Fusedale. The best features of Wether Hill, paradoxically, are found in its valleys : eastwards, Cawdale Beck and Measand Beck have attractions rarely visited except by the lone shepherd ; westwards, Fusedale Beck is fed from two wooded ravines, and here too is lovely Martindale.

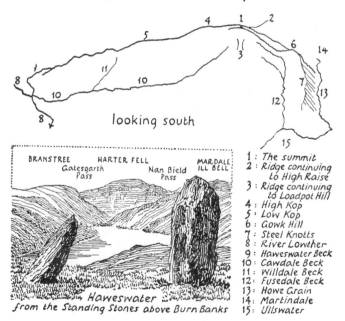

looking south

BRANSTREE   HARTER FELL   MARDALE
Gatesgarth   Nan Bield   ILL BELL
   Pass   Pass

Haweswater
from the Standing Stones above Burn Banks

1 : The summit
2 : Ridge continuing to High Raise
3 : Ridge continuing to Loadpot Hill
4 : High Kop
5 : Low Kop
6 : Gowk Hill
7 : Steel Knotts
8 : River Lowther
9 : Haweswater Beck
10 : Cawdale Beck
11 : Willdale Beck
12 : Fusedale Beck
13 : Howe Grain
14 : Martindale
15 : Ullswater

MAP

Wether Hill's slopes sprawl extensively eastwards, descending gradually in easy ridges to a wide belt of cultivated land west of the Bampton - Burn Banks road—from which the ascent will generally be commenced on this side. No details of this cultivated area are depicted on the following maps (on pages 5 and 6) other than those necessary to get the walker to the open fell as quickly as possible.

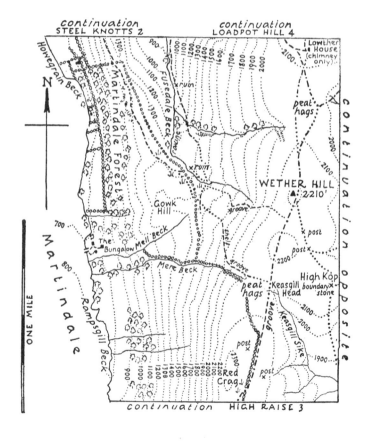

MAP

The eastern slopes of Wether Hill are
bounded on the north by Cawdale Beck
and on the south by Measand Beck, but
some detail of the adjacent fells is, in
addition, given below because they carry
routes that lead onto Wether Hill.

N

ONE MILE

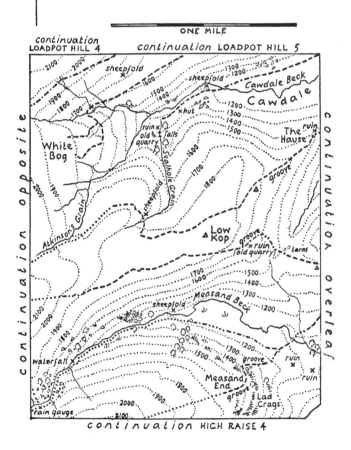

MAP

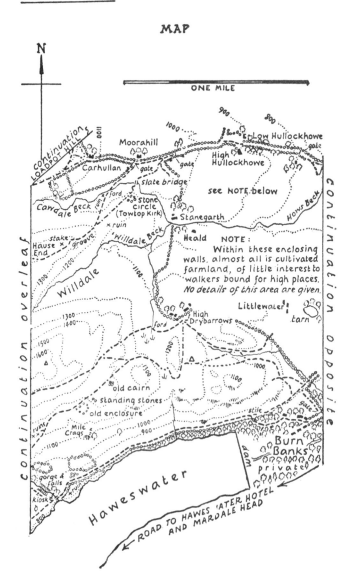

ONE MILE

NOTE:
Within these enclosing walls, almost all is cultivated farmland, of little interest to walkers bound for high places. No details of this area are given.

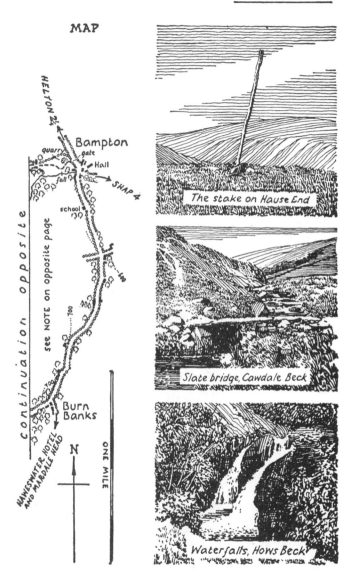

MAP

HELTON
Bampton
quarry
gate
Hall
fall
SHAP 4
school
700
continuation opposite
see note on opposite page
N
ONE MILE
Burn Banks
HAWESWATER HOTEL
AND MARDALE HEAD

The stake on Hause End

Slate bridge, Cawdale Beck

Waterfalls, Hows Beck

ASCENTS FROM HOWTOWN AND MARTINDALE
1750 feet of ascent, 3 miles, from Howtown
1550 feet of ascent, 2½ miles, from Martindale old church

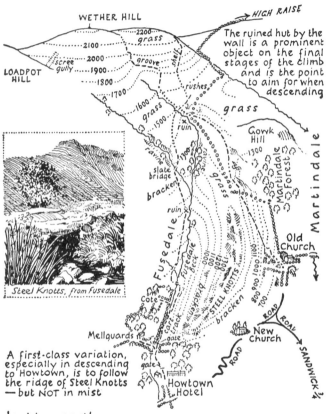

WETHER HILL

→ HIGH RAISE

2200
grass

2100

scree
gully   2000   groove   shelf

LOADPOT
HILL   1900

1800

1700   rushes

1600   grass

grass   1500   ruin

The ruined hut by the wall is a prominent object on the final stages of the climb and is the point to aim for when descending

Gowk Hill
1300

1300

ravine   1700

slate bridge

bracken

Martindale Forest

grass

Martindale

ruin ×

Fusedale

Fusedale Beck

1000   900
1200   1100

Old Church

1300

Cote

cart   track

STEEL KNOTTS

800 900 1000 1100

bracken

700

Mellguards

gate

New Church

ROAD

ROAD

gate

ROAD

SANDWICK 4½

Howtown Hotel

Steel Knotts, from Fusedale.

A first-class variation, especially in descending to Howtown, is to follow the ridge of Steel Knotts — but NOT in mist

looking south

There are many fells more worthy of climbing than Wether Hill, the final slope being very dull, but there are no more delightful starting-points than Howtown and Martindale, the approach from the latter being especially good — until the last slope is reached.

ASCENTS FROM BURN BANKS AND BAMPTON
1550 feet of ascent from Burn Banks; 1750 from Bampton.
4½ miles from Burn Banks direct, 5 via Measand Beck;
5 miles from Bampton

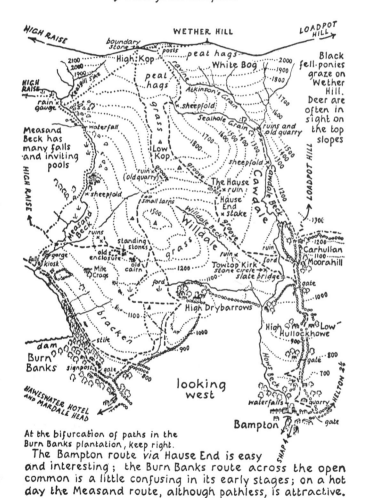

At the bifurcation of paths in the Burn Banks plantation, keep right.

The Bampton route via Hause End is easy and interesting; the Burn Banks route across the open common is a little confusing in its early stages; on a hot day the Measand route, although pathless, is attractive.

THE SUMMIT

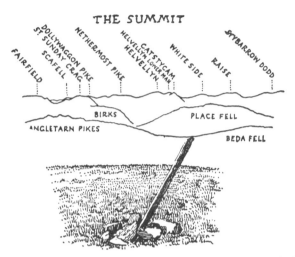

Two rounded grassy mounds of similar altitude, separated by a slight depression, form the summit. The more extensive of the two mounds, the southern, is quite featureless: the small northern mound is the recognised top and carries a wooden stake set in a small cairn (one stone of which is a boundary stone lying on its side). The summit is popular with grazing animals of various species, but humans will find it a dreary and uninteresting place. The High Street crosses the top, but along here is barely noticeable, being no more distinct than a sheep-trod.

DESCENTS: All slopes are easy, and it is a waste of time to look for the few paths. For Bampton, pass over High Kop to join one of two good grooves. For Martindale and Howtown descend west to the ruin by the prominent broken crosswall below; leave the ruin on the *right*, passing through the gateway in the wall, for Martindale; but for Fusedale and Howtown leave the ruin well to the *left*.

In mist, there is little danger of accident, but keep out of stream-beds which run in ravines.

The boundary stone, High Kop, with High Raise in the background

THE VIEW

Principal Fells

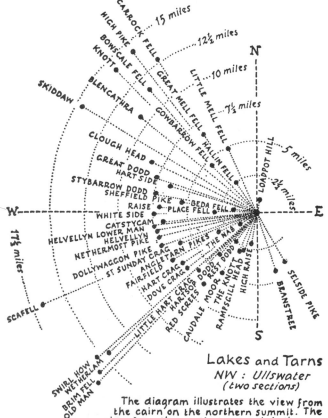

Lakes and Tarns
NW : Ullswater
(two sections)

The diagram illustrates the view from
the cairn on the northern summit. The
view from the southern summit is the same
substantially, but in addition Scafell Pike
can be seen. There is a wide prospect of the
Pennines, but undoubtedly the best feature is
the finely-grouped Helvellyn and Fairfield fells
across the rough, romantic Martindale country.

RIDGE ROUTES

To LOADPOT HILL, 2201' : 1 mile : N
Depression at 2025' : 180 feet of ascent

An easy walk, safe in mist
Keep to the left side of the depression (a faint track materialises) to avoid the peat-hags that cut deeply into the old path (the High Street) on the right side. Make a beeline for the chimney-stack ahead — the summit (quartz cairn) is directly beyond.

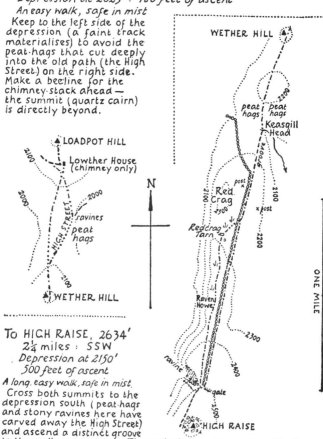

WETHER HILL

peat hags | peat hags

Keasgill Head

Red Crag

post

post

Redcrag Tarn

Raven Howe

N

LOADPOT HILL

Lowther House (chimney only)

ravines
peat hags

HIGH STREET

WETHER HILL

ONE MILE

gate

HIGH RAISE

To HIGH RAISE, 2634'
2¼ miles : SSW
Depression at 2150'
500 feet of ascent

A long, easy walk, safe in mist.
Cross both summits to the depression south (peat-hags and stony ravines here have carved away the High Street) and ascend a distinct groove to the wall-corner ahead. The route follows the wall south: it may be crossed near Redcrag Tarn for the best views, but on a gusty day it offers shelter if kept immediately on the right. When the wall ends at a short fence, above a steep ravine, the path climbs across the open fell. The cairn is among stones 100 yards away to the left of the path at its highest point.

Measand Beck The Forces of
Measand Beck,
near its outlet into Haweswater, need
no introduction to frequenters of this
area, but the waterfalls illustrated,
two miles upstream, are rarely seen.

Yoke

2309'

spelt 'Yolk' on some Ordnance Survey maps

▲ HIGH STREET

▲ ILL BELL
▲ YOKE

● Kentmere

● Troutbeck

MILES

0   1   2   3   4

from the Kirkstone-Windermere road

MAP

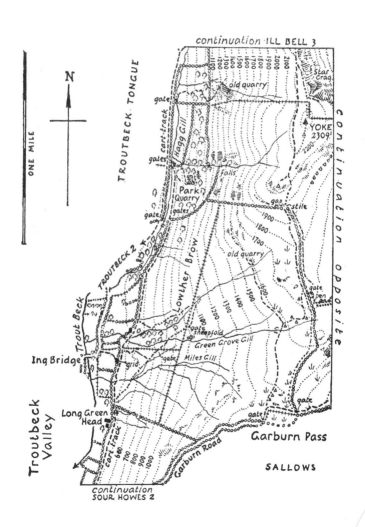

continuation ILL BELL 3

continuation opposite

TROUTBECK TONGUE

Star Crag

old quarry

gate

cart-track

Hagg Gill

YOKE
2309

gates

falls

Park
Quarry

gates

gap
stile

gate

gates

1900

1800

1700

old quarry

TROUTBECK 2

Lowther Brow

1600

1500

gate
pen

1400

1300

Trout Beck

1200

1000

gate
sheepfold

Green Grove Gill

grid

gate

Miles Gill

Ing Bridge

gate

gate

Garburn Pass

Troutbeck Valley

Long Green
Head

cart-track

600

700

800

900

1000

Garburn Road

SALLOWS

N

ONE MILE

continuation
SOUR HOWES 2

NATURAL FEATURES

Yoke is best known as the southern outpost of the Ill Bell ridge leading up to High Street from Garburn Pass, and is usually dismissed as a dull unattractive mound. As seen from Troutbeck, this seems a quite accurate assessment, but the Kentmere flank is very different, abounding in interest. On this side, below the summit, is the formidable thousand-foot precipice of Rainsborrow Crag (the safety of which is a subject of disagreement between rock-climbers and foxes) and, rising above Kentmere village, is a knobbly spur that looks like the knuckles of a clenched fist—a place of rocky excrescences, craggy tors and tumbled boulders, and a fine playground for the mountaineering novice. Both flanks of Yoke carry the scars of old quarrying operations.

grass

bracken

12

bracken

1 : The summit
2 : Garburn Pass
3 : Rainsborrow Crag
4 : Skeel Crags
5 : Buck Crag
6 : Castle Crag
7 : Piked Howes
8 : Ewe Crags
9 : Cowsty Knotts
10 : Raven Crag
11 : Badger Rock
12 : Lowther Brow
13 : Kentmere Reservoir
14 : Bryant's Gill
15 : River Kent
16 : Hall Gill
17 : Trout Beck

looking north

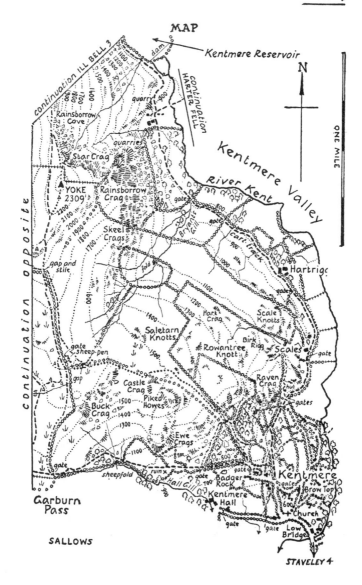

MAP

Kentmere Reservoir

N

ONE MILE

continuation ILL BELL 3

continuation HARTER FELL

Kentmere Valley

River Kent

dam

quarry

Rainsborrow Cove

quarries

Star Crag

▲ YOKE 2309

Rainsborrow Crag

Skeel's Crags

gap and stile

Bryant's Gill

Cart track

Hartrigg

gate

gate

gate

Scale Knotts

fold

Hart Crag

Saletarn Knotts

Rowantree Knott

Birk Rigg

Scales

gate

gate sheep pen

gap

Castle Crag

Buck Crag

Piked Howes

Raven Crag

hut

gates

continuation opposite

Ewe Crags

gate

sheepfold

Hall Gill

ruin x

gate

Badger Rock

Kentmere Hall

gate

Kentmere

gate

Brow Top

Church

Low Bridge

gate

gate

Garburn Pass

SALLOWS

STAVELEY 4

ASCENT FROM GARBURN PASS
850 feet of ascent : 1¾ miles

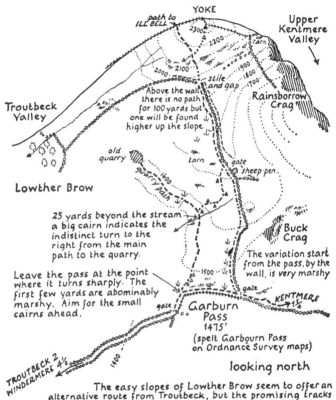

YOKE

path to
ILL BELL

2300

2200

Upper
Kentmere
Valley

tarn

2100

2000   2100

1900

1800

1700

stile
and gap

Rainsborrow
Crag

Troutbeck
Valley

Above the wall
there is no path
for 100 yards but
one will be found
higher up the slope

old
quarry

tarn

gate
sheep pen.

quarry path

1600

Lowther Brow

Buck
Crag

25 yards beyond the stream
a big cairn indicates the
indistinct turn to the
right from the main
path to the quarry.

The variation start
from the pass, by the
wall, is very marshy.

1500

Leave the pass at the point
where it turns sharply. The
first few yards are abominably
marshy. Aim for the small
cairns ahead.

gate

gate

KENTMERE
1¾

gate   Garburn
Pass
1475'

(spelt Garbourn Pass
on Ordnance Survey maps)

1400

TROUTBECK 2
WINDERMERE 4½

looking north

The easy slopes of Lowther Brow seem to offer an
alternative route from Troutbeck, but the promising tracks
climbing through the bracken from the cart-road behind Long Green
Head (see map) do not continue far and the ascent becomes tiresome.
The route depicted here, from Garburn Pass, is better in every way.

This is a dull, easy walk, but the dreary foreground
is relieved by the splendid views to the west. There
are patches of marshy ground to the 1800' contour —
the route throughout is on grass.

ASCENT FROM KENTMERE
1800 feet of ascent : 2½ miles (3 miles via Garburn Pass)

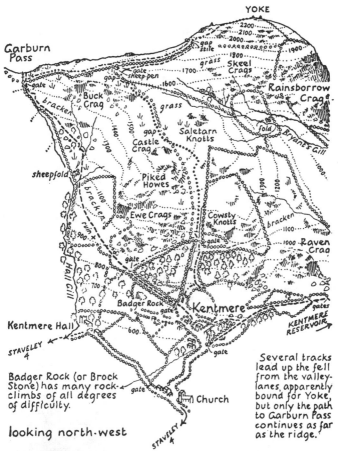

Garburn Pass

YOKE

Buck Crag

Skeel Crags

Rainsborrow Crag

Castle Crag

Saletarn Knotts

Bryant's Gill

sheepfold

Piked Howes

Ewe Crags

Cowsty Knotts

Raven Crag

Hall Gill

Badger Rock

Kentmere

Kentmere Hall

KENTMERE RESERVOIR

STAVELEY 4

Badger Rock (or Brock Stone) has many rock-climbs of all degrees of difficulty.

looking north-west

Church

STAVELEY 4

Several tracks lead up the fell from the valley-lanes, apparently bound for Yoke, but only the path to Garburn Pass continues as far as the ridge.

Although Garburn Pass offers the easiest route, the craggy screen rising steeply behind the village will tempt the more adventurous walker : the top of the spur is a maze worth exploring, but only the route depicted guarantees to avoid unclimbable walls.

THE SUMMIT

ILL BELL   HIGH STREET   MARDALE ILL BELL

The highest point on the broad grassy top is a small rock-sided platform with a cairn. A wire fence forms a right-angle nearby. Another cairn (a better viewpoint) stands 130 yards to the south.

DESCENTS: A short descent down the western slope brings into view a good track skirting the summit: this, followed to the left (south) leads to the wall that goes down to Garburn Pass.

In mist, note that the north-east and east slopes are entirely dangerous, and that the lower western flank is very rough: it features, in a walled enclosure, the bracken-concealed, fearful abyss of Park Quarry, a fall into which would definitely end the day's walk. From the top cairn, descend west (170 yards only) to the track; or, if uncertain of the compass points, follow the wire fence left, and left again at another angle — the track will be picked up as it crosses the fence at a broken stile. Turn left (south) along the track, which becomes indistinct but points the direction of the wall going down to Garburn Pass.

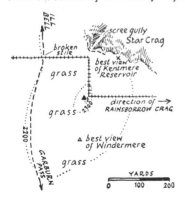

ILL BELL

broken stile

scree gully
Star Crag

grass

best view of Kentmere Reservoir

grass 2200

direction of RAINSBORROW CRAG

best view of Windermere

2200

GARBURN PASS

grass

YARDS
0   100   200

Park Quarry — in the sheltered depths of which flowers bloom and ferns flourish in December

THE VIEW

This is a good viewpoint, more particularly for the wide sweep of country and sea southwards. Of the Lakeland scene, the prospect due west is especially attractive.

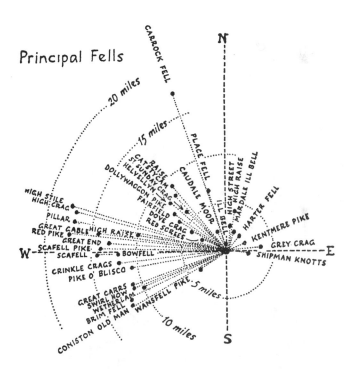

Principal Fells

Lakes and Tarns

SSW : *Windermere* (much better seen from the south cairn : a very beautiful view)

SW : *Blelham Tarn*
———— To see *Kentmere Reservoir*, visit the edge of Star Crag, where the reservoir comes suddenly and dramatically into view north-east

RIDGE ROUTE

To ILL BELL, 2476' : ⅔ mile : N
Depression at 2180' : 300 feet of ascent
An easy climb, safe in mist

Cross the fence and proceed down to and across the depression with the escarpment close by on the right. This is a simple walk in clear weather, but, although there is no difficulty in mist, it may then be not quite easy to get safely off the top of Ill Bell.

HALF A MILE

Raven Crag

Buck Crag

Badger Rock
(Brock Stone)

West face　　　　　　　　　　　*East face*

This isolated rock stands within fifty yards of the Garburn path, just beyond the last buildings of Kentmere. A well-known local landmark, it has little fame outside the valley. Although the base of the rock is now silted up, there is little doubt that it is a boulder fallen from the fellside above, a theory supported by the cavities beneath (a refuge for foxes), and it may well be the biggest boulder in Lakeland. There are rock-climbs on it of all degrees of difficulty.

Rainsborrow Crag

THE FAR EASTERN FELLS
Some Personal Notes
in conclusion

It would be very remiss of me if I did not take this first opportunity publicly to acknowledge, with sincere gratitude, the many kind and encouraging letters that followed the publication of Book One. There have also been offers of hospitality, of transport (I have no car nor any wish for one), of company and of collaboration, and of financial help — all of which I have declined as gracefully as I could whilst feeling deeply appreciative, for I am stubbornly resolved that this must be a single-handed effort. I have set myself this task, and I am pigheaded enough to want to do it without help. So far, everything is all right. Sufficient copies of Book One were sold to pay the printer's bill, and here again I must thank all readers who recommended the book to others, for it is perfectly clear that, lacking full facilities for publicity and distribution, it could hardly have succeeded otherwise.

I have just completed the last page of Book Two, and feel like a man who has come home from a long and lonely journey. Rarely did I meet anyone on my explorations of the High Street fells. Usually I walked from morning till dusk without a sight of human beings. This is the way I like it, but what joys have been mine that other folk should share! Let me make a plea for the exhilarating hills that form the subject of this book. They should not remain neglected. To walk upon them, to tramp the ridges, to look from their tops across miles of glorious country, is constant delight. But the miles are long, and from one place of accommodation to another they are many. The Far Eastern Fells are for the strong walker and should please the solitary man of keen observation and imagination. Animal and bird life is much in evidence, and not the least of the especial charms of the area is the frequent sight of herds of ponies and deer that make these wild heights their home.

Perhaps I have been a little unkind to Manchester Corporation in referring to Mardale and Swindale in this book. If we can accept as absolutely necessary the conversion of Haweswater, then it must be conceded that Manchester have done the job as unobtrusively as possible. Mardale is still a noble valley. But man works with such clumsy hands! Gone for ever are the quiet wooded bays and shingly shores that Nature had fashioned so sweetly in the Haweswater of old; how aggressively ugly is the tidemark of the new Haweswater! A cardinal mistake has been made, from the walker's point of view, in choosing the site for the new hotel: much more convenient would have been a re-built Dun Bull at the head of the valley, or better still amongst the trees of The Rigg. For a walker who can call upon transport, however, the new road gives splendid access to the heart of the fells.

I leave this area to renew acquaintance with the more popular and frequented heights in the middle of Lakeland — the Langdale, Grasmere and Keswick triangle. This is a beautiful part of the district, and I shall enjoy it; but it is a weakness of mine to be for ever looking back, and often I shall reflect on the haunting loneliness of High Street and the supreme loveliness of Ullswater. It will please me then to think that this book may perhaps help to introduce to others the quiet delights that have been mine during the past two years.

Autumn, 1956   A.W.